Moral Action in a Complex World:
Franciscan Perspectives

Washington Theological Union
Symposium Papers
2008

© Franciscan Institute Publications
St. Bonaventure University
St. Bonaventure, NY   14778
2008

CFIT/ESC-OFM Series
Number 8

The articles in this book were originally presented
at a symposium sponsored by the Franciscan Center
at Washington Theological Union, Washington, DC,
May 23-25, 2008

This publication is the eighth in a series of documents
resulting from the work of the
Commission on the Franciscan Intellectual Tradition
of the English-speaking Conference of the Order of Friars Minor.
(CFIT/ESC-OFM)

Cover design: Jennifer L. Davis

ISBN10: 1-57659-154-9
ISBN13: 978-1-57659-154-3

Library of Congress Control Number
2008944178

Printed and bound in the United States of America

BookMasters, Inc.
Ashland, Ohio

TABLE OF CONTENTS

ABBREVIATIONS

WRITINGS OF SAINT FRANCIS

Adm	The Admonitions
BlL	A Blessing for Brother Leo
CtC	The Canticle of the Creatures
CtExh	The Canticle of Exhortation
LtAnt	A Letter to Brother Anthony of Padua
1LtCl	First Letter to the Clergy (Early Edition)
2LtCl	Second Letter to the Clergy (Later Edition)
1LtCus	The First Letter to the Custodians
2LtCus	The Second Letter to the Custodians
1LtF	The First Letter to the Faithful
2LtF	The Second Letter to the Faithful
LtL	A Letter to Brother Leo
LtMin	A Letter to a Minister
LtOrd	A Letter to the Entire Order
LtR	A Letter to Rulers of the Peoples
ExhP	Exhortation to the Praise of God
PrOF	A Prayer Inspired by the Our Father
PrsG	The Praises of God
OfP	The Office of the Passion
PrCr	The Prayer before the Crucifix
ER	The Earlier Rule (Regula non bullata)
LR	The Later Rule (Regula bullata)
RH	A Rule for Hermitages
SalBVM	A Salutation of the Blessed Virgin Mary
SalV	A Salutation of Virtues
Test	The Testament

EARLY BIOGRAPHICAL SOURCES

1C	The Life of Saint Francis by Thomas of Celano
2C	The Remembrance of the Desire of a Soul
LJS	The Life of Saint Francis by Julian of Speyer
1MP	The Mirror of Perfection (Smaller Version)
2MP	The Mirror of Perfection (Larger Version)
ScEx	The Sacred Exchange
AP	The Anonymous of Perugia
L3C	The Legend of the Three Companions
AC	The Assisi Compilation
LMj	The Major Legend by Bonaventure

FA:ED	*Francis of Assisi: Early Documents*, ed. Regis Armstrong, Wayne Hellmann, William Short, three volumes (New York: New City Press, 1999, 2000, 2001)

PREFACE

Francis of Assisi, often referred to as a vernacular theologian, was at the center of that perfect storm known as the Franciscan Movement. While the Order's roots are unmistakably lay it quickly became established as a clerical organ of the thirteenth century Roman Catholic Church and, as such, was often at the forefront of theological and philosophical debate affecting every aspect of the faith life of that time. Leaders from within the Order rose up to guide the development of those discussions and to safeguard the orthodoxy of the faithful. Names like Anthony of Padua, Alexander of Hales, Bonaventure of Bagnoregio, John Duns Scotus, Peter John Olivi and William of Ockham – to mention just a few – have come down to us and their arguments continue to entice us into that world of subtlety and complexity which was Medieval Scholasticism.

Scholars, both within the Family and without, search the teachings and writings of these medieval giants for insights that can be applied to contemporary challenges. It is just that which has drawn us to Washington Theological Union this May of 2008: the opportunity to engage with these medieval philosophers and theologians on the topic of moral decision-making and the relevance of these thirteenth and fourteenth century Franciscans to today's world and today's Church.

This present volume presents the thought of five of the foremost scholars on that very topic: moral decision-making. We begin with the work of Brian Johnstone who takes up the issue of what features of the twenty-first century could pose challenges for decision making? Avoiding the temptation to list those issues where difficult decisions are clearly needed, – for example, peace, hunger, AIDS, ecology and global warming – he, instead focuses on the question of "methods" and offers a framework within which these issues can be addressed. Constructing an appropriate way of approaching contemporary issues is, perhaps, the most important challenge that we have to face.

Our second presenter is Thomas Shannon who helps us explore perspectives on human nature offered by our Franciscan tradition. These perspectives present a profound challenge to our contemporary American way of life. First, it challenges the way we act with respect to nature. Second, the Franciscan vision challenges how we view ourselves and others. Third, it challenges how we view the dignity of human beings. Stemming from creation in the image of God, our dignity is a vocation. And the vocation consists in our being the voice of creation. By this vocation we participate in the transformation of the world and thus join in the cosmic praise to the resurrected and glorified Christ.

Our third presenter, Kathryn Getek, begins her investigation of virtue with Christ's suffering and leads us to understand virtue's aim is arriving at delight in God. She reflects on the reality of Franciscan virtue as counterpointing specific Franciscan vices and leads us to new ways to think about applying the virtues of Francis and Clare to our own lives. Getek suggests a way of integrating the traditional cardinal virtues and the Aristotelian mean with the spiritual teachings of Bonaventure and John of Caulibus. She suggests, as particularly Franciscan, a version of the traditional cardinal virtues: Franciscan justice found in humility, Franciscan fortitude in patience, Franciscan temperance in poverty, and Franciscan prudence in relational and affective discretion. Ultimately, any discussion of Franciscan virtue, to be authentic, must be concerned not with human development or happiness but with praise of and delight in God.

Thomas Nairn, our fourth presenter, looks at the question of whether death is a moral issue. In his presentation he travels a circuitous route from the theological and medical viewpoints of the Middle Ages to the complex issues of today's advanced medical care and the end-of-life experience complicated by society's dependence on legal remedies. The Catholic ethical tradition regarding the end of life prides itself in being an ethic of care. A conversation between the Franciscan intellectual tradition and Catholic bioethics can, however, clarify the true meaning of care.

Rooted in the Middle Ages, the Franciscan tradition has not equated care with the prolongation of life. The Franciscan intellectual tradition arose at a time when to prolong life was seen as immoral, evidence of an attachment to life that was still "sinfully loved." The Franciscan intellectual tradition thus raises larger questions regarding the nature and complexity of care for the dying. As the trend in modern bioethics seems to equate the "medical good" with what is truly good for a patient, perhaps the Franciscan intellectual tradition can become a renewed source for discussions about what constitutes appropriate medical interventions and end of life care.

Mary Beth Ingham begins the final presentation in this series with a feminist critique of contemporary moral philosophy. Searching for an appropriate foundation for an understanding of the moral person, Ingham integrates the views of feminist thinkers with Scotus's thought and identifies the moral person as the agent and object of love and care. Scotus's vision is both personal and creative. The moral person is not an autonomous agent but a member of community which is affected deeply by choices and actions of its members. Scotus's theory calls for the highest level of personal development and intellectual training of the individual to promote the necessary sensitivity to the beauty around and to encourage creative responses in specific situations. In this way, Scotus's approach to moral decision-making may provide what is needed for a renewed moral discussion today: a moral foundation based on love and beauty, moral judgment as a discerning of goodness and beauty, and moral action as giving birth to beauty, in the agent and in the world.

Scotus the Franciscan, seeing the moral order as going beyond the individual self to point toward communion and relationship, with others but ultimately with God, understands participation in divinity as the true human goal. This goal is a deep relationship of love based upon the nature of God as source of reality. Relationship is the moral goal because the divine is essentially relational, because we are created in the image of God, and because we are invited to enter freely into that relationship. This type of Trinitarian foundation has clear implications for an environmental ethic as well.

So our presenters have engaged us in a challenging discussion of how our Franciscan tradition can give direction to and enrich our own moral development in our twenty-first century context. It is now up to us to plumb their thought and take it to the next level: integration in our own thinking and experience in whatever ways will lead us to that delight in God and eventual absorption into the Trinitarian relationship of love which is our true and blessed end.

Daria Mitchell, O.S.F.
Franciscan Institute

MORAL DECISION MAKING IN THE 21ST CENTURY: METHODS AND CHALLENGES

BRIAN JOHNSTONE, C.Ss.R.

In this presentation I am going to suggest that the experience of receiving and giving is the primary moral experience and thus the source of a moral theology that could respond to the challenges of our age. This would be a moral theology of love, not a formless love, but a love whose inner logic would be that of receiving and giving gifts. This way of approaching the topic suggests a connection with the Franciscan tradition and I will develop this in the course of my essay.

I shall be invoking the thought of the French Philosopher, Jean-Luc Marion and in particular his philosophy of givenness as developed in his many works, in particular in *Being Given: Towards a Phenomenology of Givenness*.[1] Marion is a French philosopher, recognized as a leading Catholic thinker, who is Director of Philosophy at the University of Paris IV (Sorbonne). He is currently the John Nuveen Professor of the Philosophy of Religion and Theology at the University of Chicago Divinity School; also in the Department of Philosophy and the Committee on Social Thought at the same university. He is regarded by some as a key contributor to a postmodern theology. The tension between reason/being and love/gift, and the attribution of priority to the latter, that we

---

[1] Jean-Luc Marion, *Being Given: Towards a Phenomenology of Givenness*, trans. Jeffrey Kosky (Stanford: Stanford University Press, 2002).

find in Marion's work would recall, of course, the differences between the Thomist tradition, (the primacy of reason and being) and the Franciscan tradition (the primacy of love and the good). It would seem that Marion's thinking is closer to the Franciscan tradition.

Marion's thought in his work, *God Without Being*, has been interpreted by Thomas Carlson as implying that, "Theology needs to cease being modern theology in order to become again theology like the theologies of such ancient and medieval Christian Platonists as Pseudo-Dionysius and Bonaventure.[2] Marion's more recent work has been more philosophical than theological; he is concerned to show that his work is genuinely philosophy and not a kind of disguised theology, but theological issues are still important to him. I shall now try to follow through the "Franciscan" theme of the centrality of love and the good in relation to Marion's thinking.

At this basic level, there is an important issue for Marion. According to St. Thomas, "... the good does not add anything to being [the *ens*] either really or conceptually, *nec re nec ratione* (neither in reality nor in thought)." In Marion's view, St. Thomas here takes a position "... that is directly opposed to the anteriority, more traditionally accepted in Christian theology, of the good over the *ens*." Bonaventure, however, according to Marion, still holds the traditional position and sees the last instance that permits a contemplation of God as contained in goodness.[3] In *God without Being*, there follows a brief, highly compressed commentary on Bonaventure's *Itinerarium Mentis in Deum*.[4] From this there emerges the no-

---

[2] Marion, *God without Being*, trans. Thomas A. Carlson (Chicago: The University of Chicago Press, 1995), xii.

[3] Marion, *God without Being*, 74.

[4] Bonaventure of Bagnoregio, *Itinerarium* VI, 1. The English translation is from *Itinerarium Mentis in Deum*, with an Introduction and Commentary by Philotheus Boehner, O.F.M., WSB II (St. Bonaventure, NY: The Franciscan Institute, 1956), 89: "Having considered the essential attributes of God, we must raise the eyes of our intelligence to the contuition of the most Blessed Trinity, so as to place the second Cherub opposite the first. Now just as being itself is the principal root of the vision of the essential attributes of God as well as the name through which the others become known, so the good itself is the principal foundation of the contemplation

tion that God can be thought of as the one who gives the gift of being, and hence is prior to being. What is central here, is the act or gesture of giving the gift of being.[5] Thus, we might say that God is to be thought of as the giver of being, in an act of love, while being itself would be understood as given being and the ultimate horizon of understanding as active giving and receiving.

With a view to constructing a theology appropriate for our present century, we could translate the neo-Platonic notion of divine "emanations" into terms that would be more intelligible in our culture, such as "the divine act of giving." Similarly, the phrase from *pseudo*-Dionysius used by Bonaventure, "Good is diffusive of itself," could be rendered: "The person who is giving, gives the good gift, which is the self of the giver." It is on these lines that I suggest that the Franciscan tradition, as read by Marion, and further developed, might provide us with a basic framework for moral theology and so for moral decision making. These refined speculations may well seem to be far removed from the moral decision making that is the topic of this article. However, I would argue that decision making can only be meaningful within a framework; what I am suggesting here is that the framework should be the receiving and giving of gifts. The ultimate decision that a person must make is to choose to be a receiver of God's gifts and so become capable of giving gifts to others, or not to choose to receive gifts and so become incapable of giving. Thus, the primary sin of Adam and Eve would be interpreted as a refusal to receive the gifts of God, and idea that is to be found in the works of St. Anselm.[6]

---

of the emanations." The term "contuition" belongs in Bonaventure's theory of certain knowledge: this includes knowledge of contingent realities and the eternal ideas: the two are contuita.

[5] Marion, *God without Being*, 75.

[6] St. Anselm wrote: "... it is in the natural and willful propagation of humanity that men and women pass on to their offspring the evils which Adam brought upon himself when he rejected the good things that he had received from God." *De conceptu virginali et de originali peccato*, in *S. Anselmi Opera Omnia*, ed. F. S. Schmitt, vol. 2, (Rome: Ex officina Sansaini et

To take up now the particular topic assigned to me, what features of the twenty first century, so far, could pose challenges for our decision making? I will not attempt to list those issues where difficult decisions are clearly needed, such as for example, peace, hunger, AIDS, ecology and global warming. Rather I will take up the question of "methods" and offer a framework within which we could approach these issues.[7] Constructing an appropriate way of approaching contemporary issues, is perhaps, the most important challenge that we have to face.

The argument is a basically very simple.[8] Most people like to receive gifts, and likewise most like to give gifts, or if they do not, they recognize that it is good to receive and to give gifts. The giving of gifts and the receiving of gifts are the most basic form of human exchange without which the human race could not exist. The giving of gifts can be an expression of love and so we could put another turn on the argument: most persons want to receive love and most want to give love, so the "nature" of love could provide the basis for a common ethic. Such an ethic would not be primarily a set of laws and norms imposed by obligation, but the cultivated art of the free giving and receiving of true gifts, sustained by the structures of justice that are required to make possible and protect the free giving of gifts.

Soc, 1940), 11, 153-54, cited in Sarah Jane Boss, ed., *Mary: The Complete Resources*, (New York: Oxford University Press, 2007), 214.

[7] The notion of "framework," I take from Charles Taylor, *Source of the Self: The Making of the Modern Identity* (Cambridge, MA: Harvard University Press, 1989), 16.

[8] Marion has not developed his thought in the area of morals or ethics and has said recently that he does not intend to do so. His *Prologomena to Charity*, trans. Stephen Lewis (New York: Fordham University Press, 2002) while not a work of "moral theology," would have much to offer to this discipline. What follows here are my attempts to draw from Marion's reflections so as to shape a framework for moral theology. An extended treatment of the relation of Marion's work to ethics is Gerard McKenny, "Jean-Luc Marion and the Horizon of Modern Morality," in *Counter-Experiences: Reading Jean-Luc Marion*, ed. Kevin Hart (Notre Dame: University of Notre Dame Press, 2007), 339-55.

It would be an ethics of "reason," but reason would be understood in this context as primarily practical reason shaped by the inner logic of receiving and giving gifts. Perhaps it could be suggested that this logic would derive from the "metaphysics of love," a term, I believe, that St. Bonaventure employed. Of course, we cannot love something or someone that we do not know, as St. Thomas says, " ... the intellect moves the will." But he also says the will moves the intellect to act since the truth which is the object of the intellect, is also the good sought by the will.[9] Thus, it is not the case that a loveless knowledge must come before love. It is rather that because we want to love, we want to know someone or something to love; the desire to love requires knowledge of the one to be loved and knowledge of the gift to be given to that one as the expression of love.

This view of the relationship between reason and love might be read as signaling a new approach to the old differences between the Thomist tradition (which is said to accord primacy to reason) and the Franciscan tradition (according primacy to love) and this will indeed be taken up in the following argument. This would be particularly appropriate in this Franciscan symposium. What I propose to do is to develop the ethic of givenness with the Catholic tradition. However, if we are to develop a framework for decision making in the twenty-first century, we will need to engage with traditions other than the Catholic. Thus, while developing a framework within the Catholic tradition, we would also need to offer this to members of other traditions. But I will not undertake that second task here. However, we cannot develop an understanding of our own tradition without considering how certain cultural events have engendered internal tensions within that tradition. Hence, we need to consider some of the challenges presented to us by the twenty-first century.

There are two broad cultural and economic currents that we have inherited from the last century that have engendered much tension in the Catholic tradition; one is "post-

---

[9] *Summa Theologica* I-II, 9, 1.

modernism," the other is globalization.[10] Within the limits of this presentation, I will limit the discussion to the first. There is of course much dispute as to what "postmodern" means and when it began; some say that it is already of the past and that we are now in the post-post modern era. However, we could sum up the characteristic mark of this cultural phenomenon as "fragmentation," in the sense that the great, unifying narratives that, for many, offered a meaning and direction for human life have disintegrated.

For the Catholic Tradition, at present, there are several instances of "fragmentation" that are particularly troubling; the first is "relativism," which could be read as a "fragmentation" of doctrinal and moral traditions; this has become a major theme in the discourses of Pope Benedict XVI.[11] Another instance of the fragmentation of tradition is the phenomenon of "supermarket" Catholicism, where persons who continue to identify themselves as Catholics choose those doctrines they prefer, while rejecting others. The unified belief system of the Catholic tradition is fragmented in this way by individual choice. Kathryn Tanner finds that religious traditions in our age are no longer integrated wholes, but are fragmented.[12] Another, related movement is the critique of "reason" in postmodern philosophy.

I will first take up the issue of "relativism." Since relativism has a special relevance for moral decision-making, I will offer some brief remarks on the theme. There are two kinds of relativism: "historical relativism" holds that moral principles and norms, while they are valid or may be valid, within particular historical periods, are not so for all such periods. The second kind is cultural relativism, which holds that principles and norms may be valid for some particular cultural settings, but cannot claim to be valid for all cultures,

---

[10] Kevin Hart, *Postmodernism: a Beginner's Guide* (London: Oneworld Publications, 2004).

[11] Joseph Ratzinger and Marcello Pera, *Without Roots: The West, Relativism, Christianity, Islam*, trans. Michael F. Moore (New York: Basic Books, 2006).

[12] Kathryn Tanner, *Theories of Culture: A New Agenda for Theology* (Minneapolis, MN: Augsburg Fortress Publishers, 1997).

that is they cannot be universal.[13] It is not difficult to refute relativism of either kind: if theories or ethical systems are valid only in particular historical eras, then "relativism" can be valid for a particular period only. It cannot claim to be a universal theory. Similarly, if relativism of the second kind, holds that systems are valid only for particular cultural contexts, then relativism can be valid only for particular contexts. Such counter arguments may indeed work well in apologetic debate, but relativists do not seem to be convinced. The real difficulty is the lack on a positive alternative to relativism that can sustain claims to universality. In this presentation, I will propose such an alternative; the suggestion will be that love expressed in the receiving and giving of gifts may enable us to construct a framework to deal with relativism.

I turn now to the challenge to "reason." The challenge is directed in the first place against the "reason" of the Enlightenment with its claim to provide a foundation for all thought, but it extends more widely to a challenge all forms of reason, and in, particular, metaphysics, by which is meant any system of thought that claims to capture all reality in a system of concepts or categories, whether they be those of Aristotle, Kant, St. Thomas Aquinas, or anyone else. The claim is that such categories are "'totalizing;'" they are like a narrow procrustean bed into which reality is forced, inevitably excluding the "other, " which does not fit into the confines of these categories. A system of moral principles and norms that claim to be based on a universal "reason," such as the "natural law" upheld in the Catholic tradition, would be a prime target of such a critique. According to these critics, universal "reason" is simply not available, in particular, there can be no universal natural law based on reason, so that Catholic moral teaching on such issues as stem cells, the cloning of embryos, etc., has no basis, and merely reflects a particular, religious view.

---

[13] Eberhard Schockenhoff, *Natural Law & Human Dignity*, trans. Brian McNeil (Washington, DC: The Catholic University of America Press, 2003), 42.

One feature of postmodern culture is that it is "tolerant" in the sense that a postmodern person is prepared to respect an "other" perspective – even a "religious" perspective. A postmodernist might say, "I recognize your view that there are universal moral principles based on reason, I respect that view, but it is only your opinion. Further, your view is based on your religious convictions. I respect these, but you cannot expect me to accept them, or to allow them to play any part in public ethical discussion." But beyond this, there is the more basic issue: how do Catholics (and other believing Christians) explain to themselves why they hold their ethical principles and norms. Someone might respond, of course, that she or he believes that some moral principles and values are "true" because the Bible says so. But there is at least one difficulty here: the Bible does not deal with many of the moral questions that we have to face today. If we seek to "apply" the teaching of the Bible, it seems we have to use "reason" in some way. Or, some one might say that she believes in the moral values and principles taught by the Magisterium of the Church, because the Pope teaches this doctrine and the Pope is guided by the Holy Spirit. It is not possible to discuss all the issues involved here and a short answer will have to suffice: It is the Pope himself who has been insisting on the necessary role of reason.[14]

It is, of course, not possible to "prove" that reason is reliable, because we would have to use reason in constructing such a proof and in doing so we would have to accept the validity of reason. We have to "believe" in reason if we are to conduct any reasoned inquiry at all and we have to believe in reason if we are to discern what would be a genuine gift to another. But such a faith is not a blind and arbitrary faith: it is supported by a reasoned understanding of the giving of gifts and of love which expresses itself in the giving of gifts. Reason enables us to discern and to give true gifts and it is thus that we can know that our reasoning is valid when it guides us to the giving of true gifts. According to the logic of

---

[14] Pope Benedict XVI, Faith, Reason and the University Memories and Reflections, University of Regensburg, Tuesday, September 12, 2000.

love, expressed in the receiving and giving of gifts, a "true gift" would be one which could be freely accepted by the receiver in such a way that the receiver would become capable of freely giving to others, and, in so doing, be "fulfilled." But, of course, this suggestion calls for explanation.

THE GIFT

At this point of the argument, I turn again to the theme of gift; I offer a summary of the theme insofar as it is related to the theme of this essay. I have adapted some of Marion's ideas and suggested further implications; I do not claim that the proposals that I have drawn from his writings would all be accepted by Marion. Marion argues that, in our present cultural context, the viable way of knowing is love and he thus engages in an analysis of love as a way of knowing.[15] Marion rejects "metaphysics" as a form of knowledge,[16] and "being," as a category, in particular, as ways of knowing God. In their place, he proposes the "horizon" of givenness: it is within this horizon, opened by phenomenology, that we can know.[17] It has been alleged in criticism of Marion's thought that in his concern to attain givenness, the pure gift, free from all connotation of exchange, Marion has left behind those structures of giving; the giver, the recipient and the gift, without which giving is unintelligible.[18] Marion, however, has rejected this criticism.[19] Thus, the horizon of givenness is to be understood in terms of the structure of giver, receiver and gift. This is important for my own proposal, since the structure, giver, receiver, and gift, are essential to the argument. It has also

---

[15] "Contrary to what metaphysics has ended up claiming, love lacks neither reason nor logic; quite simply, it does not admit reason or logic other than its own." Jean-Luc Marion, *The Erotic Phenomenon*, trans. Stephen E. Lewis (Chicago: The University of Chicago Press), 217.

[16] Hart, "Introduction," 30.

[17] Marion, *Being Given*, 7.

[18] Joseph S. O'Leary, "The Gift: A Trojan Horse in the Citadel of Phenomenology?" in *Givenness and God: Questions of Jean-Luc Marion* (New York: Fordham University Press, 2005), 152.

[19] Personal communication from Marion, Friday, May 30, 2008.

been claimed that the "horizon of givenness" seems to fulfill the role of "metaphysics" despite Marion's critique of metaphysics. Be that as it may, I propose that we could find here a new way of thinking "metaphysics," according to which "being" is considered not merely as "actuality," as it was by some Thomists, but as "received and given being." The notion of being as given being is present in the thought of St. Thomas, on creation, although it is not emphasized.[20] But to say that being is created is to imply that it is given.

The notion that being is given being is much more explicit in *pseudo*-Dionysius as interpreted by Marion: "God gives Being to beings only because he precedes not only these beings, but also the gift that he delivers to them-to-be."[21] Marion himself insists that what he is doing is philosophy not theology and he rejects the criticism that he is smuggling in theological notions under the guise of philosophical reason. However, for believers who begin with faith, it is not difficult to see how, in the light of belief in a creator, who gives being, being itself would indeed by understood as given being.

Theologically, the same line of thought could bring us to the source of all giving and receiving in the Trinity, a theme that is found in the Patristic tradition, as expressed, for example by St. Hilary of Poitiers in his *Treatise on the Trinity*. Hilary writes: "Nothing is wanting in this flawless union; in Father, Son and Holy Spirit, there is infinity of endless being, perfect reflection of the divine image, and mutual enjoyment of the gift."[22] Further, the Father's giving of the Son and the Son's self-giving on the Cross, from which comes the gift of the Spirit, by the risen Christ, would complete the link between the Christological and Trinitarian meaning of givenness.

---

[20] John Wipple, *The Metaphysical Thought of St. Thomas Aquinas*, (Washington: The Catholic University of America Press, 2000), 584. The context is the treatment of creation. The theme of gift is not expressly treated, but it would seem not inappropriate to interpret the creation of being as the gift of being.

[21] Marion, *God without Being*, 75.

[22] Hilarius Pictavensis, *De Trinitate*, Book 2, 1, 33, 35: *Patrologia Latina*. The Latin word for "gift" here is *munus*.

If I have understood correctly, St. Bonaventure provided a theological explanation of the role of the Father through the metaphysics of good, which he further explained in terms of the notion of good as diffusive of itself; the Son, as exemplar, mediates the reality of the Godhead, according to the metaphysics of being, while the Spirit joins the Father and the Son, according to the metaphysics of love.[23] I am suggesting that we might translate these classical notions into the terms of the giving and receiving of gifts: the Father is the good giver of the gift of being; the Son is receiver of the gift, and thereby becomes the giver of being to the Spirit; the Spirit as receiver becomes the giver of self to Father and Son in the gift of love and, we might say, the giver of the divine "self" to us, so that we receive the gift of our "selves" in receiving the gift of God's self. We could recall that for St. Thomas, the proper name of the Spirit is "Gift."[24] The horizon of givenness, or the giving and receiving of gifts, could provide a framework within which the old question of the primacy of being or good could be overcome; to the gain of moral theology.

The authors of text books that present and defend the primacy of being or the primacy of good, may, I suggest, have abstracted the notions of good and being, of love and reason out of the framework of the lived processes in which they function, that is, the framework of giving and receiving, and inserted them into a framework based on a kind of hierarchy of primary and secondary. Etienne Gilson speaks in these terms.[25] Thus, the authors dispute whether "good" or "being" is primary. Could it be suggested that it is not a question of an abstract hierarchy of being and good, but of successive steps within the ascent to contemplation, which can then flow into action. The framework within which to grasp the relation of good and being could be the expression of contemplation in the active life and, in particular, in receiving and giving. In this context it is the relation between good and being that is important, rather than the primacy of one or the other.

---

[23] See note 4 above.
[24] *Summa Theologica* I, q. 38, aa, 1 and 2.
[25] Marion, *God Without Being*, 217.

How then is contemplation linked with morality and decision-making? It is not possible here to enter into a discussion of the connection between the contemplative life and the active life, but I will offer a brief sketch. The Christian way of life begins with the experience of the gift of faith, which is formed by the Scriptures. There follows meditation on the Scriptures, which yields to contemplation, moving beyond concepts but still guided by the concepts of the Scriptures; this then finds expression in symbol in Liturgy and then seeks further expression in forms of reasoning, that is philosophy, to yield moral theology, which guides practical reason in the forming of decision making.[26] It is within this process that I would link contemplation with the philosophy of gift and so with practical reason exercised in decision-making.

EXPERIENCE

We can begin, as contemporary theology usually does, with experience. I have not found a discussion of the experience of giving in Marion, nor would this be expected as he seeks to transcend the psychological. However, in order to establish links between the theory of givenness, moral theology and practical decision-making, it will be helpful to include the experiential dimension. What does experience mean and which experience counts? Within the framework of givenness, the primary experience is that of receiving; the infant experiences her or his receiving from the parent food and affection and later comes to understand that she or he has received the gift of life from the parents; the parents experience giving and receiving in their self-giving to one another. The reception makes the receiver capable of giving to others. From the interpretation of the experience of giving and receiving, there emerges within the tradition further inter-

---

[26] I draw here on the accounts of the fathers and mothers of the desert, for example Evagrius Ponticus, in Simon Tugwell, O.P., *Ways of Imperfection* (Springfield, IL: Templegate, 1985), 25.

pretations of giving and receiving in the form of the different forms of love.[27]

Within the framework of receiving and giving, these forms would be interpreted somewhat differently than in the past: *Eros* love is need based love, but where the need is for that which enables one to give to another, and those qualities and virtues that one needs to become capable of giving; in friendship love, what the other desires to receive is the gift of becoming a receiver-giver, and this is what the giver desires to give to the other, so that the "ends" of the giver and the receiver, coincide in the love of friendship. *Agape* love, is expressed in a purely gratuitous giving of gifts to the other, but agape itself will require eros love, that is love concerned with the need to acquire the gift to be given and the capacity to be a giver. When the giver gives love and the other receives that love, the other, who receives, enables the giver of love to be a giver. It is in this sense that the "other" the receiver, gives the "self," that is, the self as giver, to the one who originally gives the gift of love. The phrase "self-giving" thus has a twofold sense: it can refer to the gift of "one's self" to the other; it can also refer to the gift of "self," that is what constitutes the receiver as a receiver and giver and so as a "self." One gives her/his "self" to the other, but also gives to the other, the other's self.

As Marion writes, one is first gifted, before one becomes a "self." Here Marion is challenging those philosophies which would hold that the self constitutes its own self.[28] We are not "self-made" men or women; we are receivers of the gift of selfhood. Thus we can say, and these thoughts are my interpretation of Marion, not his own words, that we are "gifted-givers," and to be a person means to be a gifted giver.

We can choose to be such a gifted giver; this is not a "creation" of our selves, since the self is something given by another, but we can affirm that selfhood. This, I would propose,

---

[27] Marion would challenge these distinctions, see *The Erotic Phenomenon*, 217.

[28] Hart, "Introduction," 16; Marion, *Being Given*, 322: "… he is himself received from what he receives."

is what the "fundamental option" would mean within the framework of givenness. Having chosen to be a gifted giver, when I recognize another as one who is to receive, in order, in turn, to become a gifted giver, that other is experienced as profoundly attractive. The other does not impose on me, in the first place, an obligation, but draws forth a response by the power of attraction. The response to attraction is the will to give, or the will to love.

However, it is possible that persons do not choose to be gifted-givers; they can choose to not receive gifts, primarily the gifts from God and also the gifts from others, and not receiving those gifts they are unable to give to others.[29] They then have to fall back on their own limited resources and, in this condition, they cannot freely receive, they can only "take" whatever they can get. If they do "give" to others, they will do so only to dominate and control those others. Such a gift is not a true gift, and such giving is not true giving, but a form of domination. This is the primal sin, the willed refusal to receive that makes one incapable of giving.

But when the choice is made to receive gifts, the inner logic of love comes into play: that logic requires that I seek to know the "nature" of the other, and the "nature" of the gift that I am drawn to give. If "metaphysics" includes knowing the nature of "things" and persons then the logic of love requires metaphysics; a conclusion that would oppose the total rejection of metaphysics. Furthermore, the logic of love also requires that I seek to know myself, since if I am to give a gift, I must know my capacities as a giver to another. Again, the inner logic of love requires that I seek to understand the "nature" of love itself, since only in the light of this knowledge can I know what "true" love is, and so give a true gift of love. Within this framework, the "natural inclinations" that St.

---

[29] We could recall the definition of free choice (*liberum arbitrium*) by Peter Lombard in his *Sentences*: "Free choice is that faculty of reason and will by which we either choose the good with the assistance of grace, or choose evil without such assistance." b. 2, dist. 24, c. 3. Cited in Servais Pinckaers, O.P., *Morality the Catholic View* (South Bend, IN: St. Augustine's Press, 2001), 38.

Thomas invokes as the basis of the natural law, namely, the natural inclinations to preserve life; to sexual intercourse and procreation and to seek truth and form community,[30] would be, in the first place, the natural inclinations of the other, the knowledge of which would enable the giver to judge what would be a true gift for that other. In the second place, they would include the inclinations of the giver, who also has to judge whether the act of giving would be such as to constitute her or him as a genuine gifted-giver.

Again, within the framework of givenness, as understood in this presentation, the notion of "true" finds its proper sense, in the first place, in the judgment that this is a "true" gift to another and that the other's gift to me, of my "self" is a true gift. A true gift is one that can be freely received by the other in such a way as to render that other capable of giving freely to others, and, in so doing, become a true "self," that is a gifted giver. Similarly, the notion of "reason" is applicable, in the first place, to the practical reason that guides the receiving and the giving of gifts.

As has been said, the logic of love, in the specific form of the logic of giving and receiving gifts requires seeking after a knowledge of the nature of the other and the nature of the gift that is to be given. Thus, we need to know what "human beings" are like in general and what kinds of gifts are appropriate for human beings. There are some things that cannot be appropriate gifts for human beings. As we read in the Gospels:

> Ask, and it will be given to you; search, and you will find; knock, and the door will be opened for you. [8]For everyone who asks receives, and everyone who searches, finds, and for everyone who knocks, the door will be opened. Is there anyone among you who, if your child asks for bread, will give a stone? Or if the child asks for a fish, will give a snake? (Matt 7:7 RSV)

---

[30] *Summa Theologica* I-II, 94, 2.

Just as there are some kinds of things that cannot be true gifts to an other, there are some kinds of "acts" in regard to an other that cannot be acts of gift-giving. Such acts could be referred to as "intrinsically evil acts," means acts that may never, in any circumstances be done: I have suggested here another way of accounting for such acts.

The logic of love, the logic of the receiving and giving of gifts, therefore, requires that we also seek an accurate knowledge of the biology and the psychology of the proposed receiver of the gift. We need to know that snake venom is lethal for beings with the biological make up that human beings have. Similarly, we need to know that human biology is such that humans cannot digest stones, but can digest bread. Thus the nature of the act of giving food in the form of bread is something that the logic of love requires to be known, if a true gift is to be given. But it is not the "teleology" or inherent purpose of giving food that provides the complete meaning of the act and its moral meaning, this comes from the inherent purpose of the act of giving and receiving in the relationship between giver, receiver and gift. The physical teleology of the act has moral significance only when that act is freely chosen by the giver and freely received by the recipient, as the expression of giving and receiving and thus as acts of love expressed through justice. The morality of the act is not to be defined only in terms of the abstract object of the act, and of the ordering of that object according to "nature." The argument here, of course, touches on an important theme of debate in Catholic moral theology, namely "natural teleology" and "physicalism."[31] Students of moral theology will recognize the issues here, but within the limits of this article, the matter cannot be pursued further.

The logic of love, expressed in giving and receiving also requires that the giving and the receiving be free. Thus, I suggest that the primary role of freedom is to be found in the freedom with which the gift is given and the corresponding freedom with which it is to be received. It is impossible that

---

[31] Steven A. Long, *The Teleological Grammar of the Moral Act* (Naples, Florida: Sapientia Press, 2007).

a true giving not be a free giving, just as it is impossible that a true reception of a gift not be free. Thus true freedom is the freedom exercised in free giving and receiving: it is not an abstract "freedom of indifference" by which is meant a freedom to choose one or other of contraries.[32] But neither is genuine freedom adequately expressed as "freedom for excellence," in the sense of a freedom ordered to the goal of individual perfection. Rather it is the freedom to give to the other, and to receive from the other: thus a freedom that is ordered first to the "perfection" or completion of the other, by the giving of the capacity to give. But, as I have suggested earlier, it is in becoming capable of giving to the other and actually giving to the other, that the giver herself or himself is "fulfilled" or, if you will, "perfected."

By reasoning according to the logic of love, that is of receiving and giving, we could express the first basic moral requirement as: give freely and gratuitously to others true gifts, that is, gifts that the other may receive freely, so as to become capable of freely giving to others again, and, in so giving, find completion as a person, that is as a gifted giver. This could be expressed more succinctly: instead of phrasing the first moral precept thus: "Good is to be done and evil avoided" it might be stated as: "True gifts are to be freely given, and gifts that have been given are not to be taken."

In conclusion, I would suggest how, in the light of these considerations, we could structure a framework for decision-making. These basic questions would have to be answered:

1) Who is God for me? The good giver of the gifts of love and being, or something else?

2) What is my basic intention? To receive gifts in order to be capable of giving gifts, or to take from others the gifts they have received?

3) What kind of moral person have I chosen to be, a gifted-giver or a taker?

---

[32] Pinckaers, *Morality,* 67.

4) What is my more immediate intention: am I intending to give a gift to the other or seeking to dominate and control the other through an apparent gift?

5) Do I have secondary intention; for example, in giving the gift, am I seeking to genuinely benefit the other or to increase my reputation with others and increase my own self-esteem?

6) Am I freely choosing to give?

7) Is the gift that I propose to give, such that the other can receive it freely?

8) Do the gift that I propose to give, and the way in which I propose to give it, correspond with the true desires or "inclinations" of the one who is to receive?

However, not all our relationships with others are conducted on the basis of gratuitous love; indeed for much of our life we engage in various forms of reciprocity, buying and selling, working and earning, producing and consuming. How does the ethic of receiving and giving apply here? The logic of love again is the key: if we are to give a gift, we must first ensure that the gift is ours to give. We must work to produce what is to be given, or we must acquire it in some way, often by buying it. But this will require the structures of justice, law and rights. Justice was, traditionally defined as a constant and perpetual will to give to another what is her or his due. What is due to the other is, in the first place, to give genuinely and that entails that what I give is mine to give and not the property of others, so that the receiver will not be caught up in conflicts over ownership, which will impede rather than promote the others capacity to give.

Further, when I have given the gift to the other, the logic of giving requires that I ensure that the other has security of possession so she or her can use and enjoy the gift, and give gifts to others. This again requires me, with others, to work to construct and maintain structures of law and rights. Rights are not things or entities that somehow just exist; rights are what we ought to construct and respect so as to make possible and protect the receiving and giving of gifts. In a sense it is correct to say that there are no "natural rights," that is rights that are somehow derived immediately from nature. Rights are structures that we ought to construct, because we are committed to the logic of giving and receiving, that is to the logic of love. But, as I have suggested earlier, the logic of love requires the knowledge and respect for the nature of persons and things.

Thus we would generate further questions to be asked: questions of justice?

1) Have I worked to obtain what is to be given as a gift, or otherwise acquired it justly?

2) Is the gift mine to give?

3) Have I so acted as to support the construction and maintenance of the social and legal structures necessary to protect and promote the receiving and giving of gifts? These structures would, of course, include the law.

4) Have I challenged and worked to change those structures which undermine the giving and receiving of gifts, and support the taking of gifts that persons have received?

5) Are the social and legal structures that I support and maintain such that the society that is constituted by those structures preserves zones of free giving and receiving, without which the further structures of exchange, ruled by justice, would have no human meaning? In short, is the kind of society I support one which promotes free giving and receiving, or one that reduces all human interaction to economic exchange?

Some examples will show how this framework of decision-making would apply. The donation of organs by a living donor to save the lives of others could be, and no doubt usually is, a genuine giving of a gift to another. But if the donation were to become a purely commercial transaction, a buying and selling, there would be no place for a genuine giver or receiver in a relationship of the giving and receiving of gifts. Such an exchange would eliminate the basic structure, giving and receiving, that constitutes the basis of human moral living. Humans are gift-receiving and gift-giving beings: to reduce them exclusively to buyers and sellers is to undermine their humanity.

There are many questions linked with globalization, but within the framework of giving and receiving gifts in a society structured by justice, the basic moral issue would be whether the process of globalization is increasingly reducing human relationships to purely economic structures of exchange. On the other hand, it may be that globalization is the most efficient way of producing and acquiring goods to be given and received.

We could consider the issue of assisted suicide within the framework that has been proposed. The most frequently discussed situation is one where a close relative is suffering from a terminal disease that is particularly painful, such as cancer of the pancreas. Although in some hospitals the palliative care provisions are inadequate, even the best palliative care cannot always eliminate all pain. A relative responsible for the care of the sick person considers the possibility of assisting the patient to die so as to cause the pain to stop. Within the framework outlined in this article, it would be necessary to consider the relationship between care-giver and patient in terms of the giving and receiving of gifts. In brief, one may not give a lethal dose to the sufferer to end the suffering, because such an act would eliminate not only the suffering but the sufferer, the receiver of the proposed "gift." In short, such an action would destroy the relationship between giver and receiver, the very basis of the human moral life.

The Human Person: Franciscan Perspectives on Contemporary Discussions

Thomas A. Shannon

Introduction

Of all the topics and issues under discussion in the last decades, surely the notion of the human person stands at the center of many of them. Whether the question is abortion, war, social justice, health care, the treatment of prisoners, or capital punishment, the person is at the center of all these debates. Critical to these discussions are the core questions: who is a person, how are we to treat persons, how do we develop as persons, how are we to act as persons? These and similar questions are at the heart of two current discussions of persons – altruism from the perspective of genetics and the nature of the person from the perspective of the transhuman or posthuman movement. These perspectives, though well developed and each with many adherents, nonetheless contain troubling perspectives and interesting ethical implications. I will address these viewpoints and then respond to them from a Franciscan perspective providing both a critique and an alternative perspective.

Two Contemporary Perspectives on the Human Person: Sociobiology and Altruism and the Transhuman Movement

Sociobiology and Altruism

Sociobiology is defined by E.O. Wilson of Harvard University as the "systematic study of the biological basis of all social behavior," a definition that suggests a high degree of continuity between animal and human behavior. Is animal behavior a model or predictor of human behavior? How do we understand the term altruism in animal behavior and then as applied humans?[1]

Though altruism describes a noble tendency in humans – actions on behalf of another with little or no regard for one's self or one's interests – in the literature of sociobiology it is near equivalent to a fighting word. Generally it refers to some form of behavior of one organism that promotes the fitness, defined narrowly as reproductive success of another, at the expense of its own fitness.

Wilson makes altruism the central theoretical problem of sociobiology. This is so because in a "Darwinist sense the organism does not live for itself. Its primary function is not even to reproduce other organisms; it reproduces genes, and it serves as their temporary carrier."[2] This occurs through natural selection "a process whereby certain genes gain representation in the following generations superior to that of other genes located at the same chromosome positions."[3] Thus the organism is but DNA's way of making more DNA, and the individual but the vehicle of the genes.

---

[1] For a fuller development of these ideas, see Thomas A. Shannon, "Human Nature in a Post-Human Genome Project World," in *Is Human Nature Obsolete?* eds., H.W. Baillie and T.K. Casey (Cambridge, MA: The MIT Press, 2005).

[2] E.O. Wilson, *Sociobiology: The Abridged Edition* (Cambridge: The Belknap Press of Harvard University, 1980), 3.

[3] Wilson, *Sociobiology*, 3.

In this context, the question is how can altruism – "self-destructive behavior performed for the benefit of others"[4] – possibly evolve through natural selection. Obviously this behavior reduces personal fitness and reproductive success and would seem to lead to the loss of the gene or genes responsible for that behavior. Wilson finds the answer to this question in kinship:

> if the genes causing the altruism are shared by two organisms because of common descent, and if the altruistic act by one organism increases the joint contribution of these genes to the next generation, the propensity to altruism will spread through the gene pool. This occurs even though the altruist makes less of a solitary contribution to the gene pool as the price of its altruistic act.[5]

Wilson argues that "the impulse need not be ruled divine or otherwise transcendental, and we are justified in seeking a more convenient biological explanation."[6] Though Wilson notes that specific forms of altruism are culturally determined, he argues that the sociobiological hypothesis "can explain why human beings differ from other mammals and why, in one narrow aspect, they more closely resemble social insects."[7]

Wilson distinguishes two forms of cooperative behavior. First is what he terms hard-core altruism: "the altruistic impulse can be irrational and unilaterally directed at others; the bestower expresses no desire for equal return and performs no unconscious actions leading to the same end."[8] Here the responses are unaffected by social reward and punishment and tend to serve the "altruist's closest relatives and

---

[4] E.O. Wilson, *On Human Nature* (Cambridge, MA: Harvard University Press, 1978), 213.

[5] Wilson, *Sociobiology*, 3.

[6] Wilson, *On Human Nature*, 153.

[7] Wilson, *On Human Nature*, 155.

[8] Wilson, *On Human Nature*, 155.

to decline steeply in frequency and intensity as relations become more distant."[9]

Second is soft-core altruism: the altruist "expects reciprocation from society for himself or his closest relatives. His good behavior is calculating...."[10] Thus soft-core altruism is essentially selfish in a traditionally moral sense as well as being influenced by cultural evolution. The psychological vehicles for this behavior are "lying, pretense, and deceit, including self-deceit, because the actor is most convincing who believes that his performance is real."[11]

In Wilson's perspective, soft-core altruism is the key to human society because it breaks the constraints on the social contract imposed by kin selection. Reciprocity is the key to the formation of society. Hard-core altruism, on the other hand, is the "enemy of civilization"[12] This favors kin selection, the favoring of one's own relatives, and permits only limited global cooperation. Thus he says,

> Our societies are based on the mammalian plan: the individual strives for personal reproductive success foremost and that of his immediate kin secondarily; further grudging cooperation represents a compromise struck in order to enjoy the benefits of group membership.[13]

This gives Wilson a basis for optimism, for he thinks humans are "sufficiently selfish and calculating to be capable of indefinitely greater harmony and social homeostasis. This statement is not self-contradictory. True selfishness, if obedient to the other constraints of mammalian biology, is the key to a more nearly perfect social contract."[14]

---

[9] Wilson, *On Human Nature*, 155.
[10] Wilson, *On Human Nature,* 155-56.
[11] Wilson, *On Human Nature*, 156.
[12] Wilson, *On Human Nature*, 157.
[13] Wilson, *On Human Nature*, 199.
[14] Wilson, *On Human Nature*, 157.

These other constraints are learning rules and emotional safeguards. Thus, honor and loyalty are reinforced while cheating, betrayal, and denial are universally rejected. Thus it seems that learning rules, based on innate, primary reinforcement, led human beings to acquire these values and not others with reference to members of their own group.... I will go further to speculate that the deep structure of altruistic behavior, based on learning rules and emotional safeguards, is rigid and universal. It generates a set of predictable group responses....[15]

Thus soft-core altruism provides the basis for various social allegiances, shifting though they may be. The critical distinction is the in-group and the out-group, the line between which fluctuates continually. But this is our social salvation for if hard-core altruism were the basis of social relations, our fate would be a continuous "intrigue of nepotism and racism, and the future bleak beyond endurance."[16] Soft-core altruism provides an optimistic cynicism that can give us the basis of a social contract. Such behavior has been "genetically assimilated and is now part of the automatically guided process of mental development."[17] Thus genes hold culture on a leash and though the leash is long, "inevitably values will be constrained in accordance with their effects on the human gene pool."[18]

Richard Dawkins, who is most popularly associated with a narrow reading of altruism through his book *The Selfish Gene*, explicitly rejects any direct application of his explanation of evolution to motives of human behavior. Yet, he describes evolution from the perspective of the gene and highlights the interest of the gene in producing replicas of itself rather than the individual as such. The choice of the metaphor of selfishness, rather than perhaps cooperation, sug-

---

[15] Wilson, *On Human Nature*, 162-63.
[16] Wilson, *On Human Nature*, 164.
[17] Wilson, *On Human Nature*, 167
[18] Wilson, *On Human Nature*, 167.

gested a motive rather than a behavior, a motive that could easily be applied to human behavior.

Even though Dawkins affirms that his focus is behavior not motive, his language certainly is open to a discussion of motives, even though there is a strong attempt to redefine such terms. Thus, in the definition of altruism as behavior "to increase another such entity's welfare at the expense of its own,"[19] welfare is understood as one's chance of survival. One looks at outcome, not motives. Thus, a selfish gene tries "to get more numerous in the gene pool. Basically the gene does this by helping to program the bodies in which it finds itself to survive and to reproduce."[20] Thus, "a gene might be able to assist replicas of itself which are sitting in other bodies. If so, this would appear as an act of individual altruism but it would be brought about by gene selfishness"[21]

The key way in which such genetically altruistic acts occur is through kin selection or within-family altruism, one that increases the greatest net benefit to one's genes, i.e., insures the highest success rate for a particular gene. As Dawkins phrases it:

> A gene for suicidally saving five cousins would not become more numerous in the population, but a gene for saving five brothers or ten first cousins would. The minimum requirement for a suicidal altruistic gene to be successful is that it should save more than two siblings (or children or parents), or more than four half-siblings (or uncles, aunts, nephews, nieces, grand- parents, grandchildren), or more than eight first cousins, etc. Such a gene, on average, tends to live on in the bodies of enough individuals saved by the altruist to compensate for the death of the altruist itself.[22]

---

[19] Richard Dawkins, *The Selfish Gene* (NY: Oxford University Press, 1976), 61.
[20] Dawkins, *The Selfish Gene*, 95.
[21] Dawkins, *The Selfish Gene*, 95.
[22] Dawkins, *The Selfish Gene*, 100.

Thus Dawkins concludes: "I have made the simplifying assumption that the individual animal works out what is best for his genes."[23]

This is essentially what Wilson calls hard core altruism and described such behavior as "the enemy of civilization."[24] Yet Dawkins sees it as the basis of reproductive success which for him is the primary agenda of evolution. Should societies emerge, well and good, but the key issue is the gene's success at getting as many copies of itself in the population as possible. The individual gene is paramount, not the individual or the society.

These perspectives seem to leave us in a rather melancholy state at best and total despair at worst. From a biological perspective, we seem to have been placed squarely in the middle of a Hobbesian world. Wilson sees the genes as keeping culture on a leash and though the leash may be long, it is nonetheless a leash. And though he sees the possibility of soft-core altruism, that, too, is kept within the confines of the genetic leash. Dawkins says that

> a predominant quality to be expected in a successful gene is ruthless selfishness.... Much as we might wish to believe otherwise, universal love and the welfare of the species as a whole are concepts which simply do not make evolutionary success.[25]

Indeed, Dawkins affirms, "I think 'nature red in tooth and claw' sums up our modern understanding of natural selection admirably."[26]

The Transhuman and Posthuman Culture

We now turn to the transhuman movement, a very interesting case study on the meaning of human nature and

---

[23] Dawkins, *The Selfish Gene*, 105.
[24] Wilson, *On Human Nature*, 157.
[25] Dawkins, *The Selfish Gene*, 2-3.
[26] Dawkins, *The Selfish Gene*, 2.

its limits.[27] Part of this movement began with the human regeneration movement whose early origins were the traditional European spas but also the Clinique La Prairie in Clarens, Switzerland operated by Dr. Paul Niehans. The primary treatment here was the injection of fetal sheep cells into humans. This movement focused on the tragedy that our bodies and death bring into human life.

> Modern transhumanism is a statement of disappointment. Transhumans regard our bodies as sadly inadequate, limited by our physiognomy, which restricts our brain power, our strength, and, the world of all our lifespan.[28]

This perspective answers with a resounding "NO" the primal question emerging from Samuel Becket's plays: "Is personal extinction worth the wait?"[29] The transhumanist disappointment with personal extinction and the "powerful vision of life as a game stacked against us all"[30] of necessity looks for solutions, but not in the traditional places, but in improvements that will come from technology, bioengineering, and genetics, with some nods to cryonics. An acronym for the movement was coined by Timothy Leary after his "turn-on, tune in, and drop out" phase: SMILE (Space Migration, I[2] – doubling of human intelligence and Life Extension).[31] And there was a countertype – MOSH (Mostly Original Substrate Humans).[32] And by means of computer jacks in one's head, one could live in a world of virtual reality and become whom-

---

[27] For a further development of these ideas, see Thomas A. Shannon, "The Transhumanist Movement: A Flawed Response to Aging and its Natural Consequences," in C. Green and M. Smyer, eds., *Aging, Biotechnology, ad the Future*, (Baltimore, MD: The Johns Hopkins University Press, 2008).

[28] Shannon, "The Transhumanist Movement."

[29] Charles Isherwoon, "A Sugarplum Vision Becomes a Taunting Specter," *The New York Times* (25 February), B2.

[30] Isherwoon, "A Sugarplum Vision."

[31] Brian Alexander, *The Rapture* (New York, NY: Basic Books, 2003), 54.

[32] Alexander, *The Rapture*, 59.

ever one wished whenever one wished. Ray Kurzweil summarizes such a vision:

> Ultimately software-based humans, albeit vastly ex-
> tended beyond the severe limitations of humans as
> we know them today, will live out on the web, project-
> ing bodies whenever they need or want them, includ-
> ing virtual bodies in diverse realms of virtual reality,
> holographically projected bodies and physical bodies
> comprised of nanobot swarms, and other forms of nan-
> otechnology.[33]

Eventually a Declaration of Extropian Principles was
generated. Extropy was the contrary of entropy and signaled
the constant improvement of humans to the point where
they became an entirely new species, in part through the assistance of various nanotechnologies that would solve most
of our problems.

THE PRINCIPLES OF EXTROPY IN BRIEF

Perpetual Progress

Extropy means seeking more intelligence, wisdom, and
effectiveness, an open-ended lifespan, and the removal of political, cultural, biological, and psychological limits to continuing development. Perpetually overcoming constraints
on our progress and possibilities as individuals, as organizations, and as a species. Growing in healthy directions without bound.

Self-Transformation

Extropy means affirming continual ethical, intellectual,
and physical self-improvement, through critical and creative

---

[33] Ray Kurzweil, "The Evolution of Mind in the Twenty-First Century,"
in George Gilder and Jay Richards, eds., *Are We Spiritual Machines?* (Se-
attle, WA: Discovery Institute Press, 2002), 51-52.

thinking, perpetual learning, personal responsibility, proactivity, and experimentation. Using technology – in the widest sense to seek physiological and neurological augmentation along with emotional and psychological refinement.

Practical Optimism

Extropy means fueling action with positive expectations – individuals and organizations being tirelessly proactive. Adopting a rational, action-based optimism or "proaction," in place of both blind faith and stagnant pessimism.

Intelligent Technology

Extropy means designing and managing technologies not as ends in themselves but as effective means for improving life. Applying science and technology creatively and courageously to transcend "natural" but harmful, confining qualities derived from our biological heritage, culture, and environment.

Open Society

Extropy means supporting social orders that foster freedom of communication, freedom of action, experimentation, innovation, questioning, and learning. Other extropian behaviors include opposing authoritarian social control and unnecessary hierarchy and favoring the rule of law and decentralization of power and responsibility. Those who prefer bargaining to battling, exchange to extortion, and communication to compulsion are also likely to seek an openness to improvement rather than a static utopia. Extropia ("ever-receding stretch goals for society") trumps utopia ("no place").

Self-Direction

Extropy means valuing independent thinking, individual freedom, personal responsibility, self-direction, self-respect, and a parallel respect for others.

Rational Thinking

Extropy means favoring reason over blind faith and questioning over dogma. It means understanding, experimenting, learning, challenging, and innovating rather than clinging to beliefs.[34]

As one reads these, it is hard not to agree with many of the sentiments expressed. Who does not value at least some degree of rationality, negotiation rather than battles, freedom, and responsibility? Yet below the surface and sometimes on the surface, the transhumanist discontent with the status quo, the rejection of limits, and the affirmation of growth without bounds emerge as salient features. A deep restlessness with the status quo and the way things are is the underlying motive to move us to our new transhuman future.

According to some in the movement, "the future belonged to molecular biology, which had the power to salve human desperation over disease and death."[35] Death was simply not to be accepted. Or as phrased by Robert Edwards, of IVF fame in England, "We are the last five minutes of evolution and we have gone wrong! Badly wrong!"[36]

As I have noted a variety of means were proposed to eliminate the problem of death: supplements, diets, exercise, computers, biotechnology, cryogenics, and possibly cloning. Additionally a great deal of sexual activity with many partners seems to be part of the equation, if one is to believe the sometimes breathless prose in the book *The Rapture* that highlights many of the activities of a select group of self-proclaimed posthumans. One also seems to need a fair amount of money to purchase the required supplies, to have the leisure time to pursue these activities, and to travel to all the Centers and conferences. Nancie Clark, who changed her name to Natasha Vita-More – to express her desire for

---

[34] Max More, Chairman, Extropy Institute http://www.extropy.com/principles.htm.

[35] More, Extropy Institute, 79.

[36] More, Extropy Institute, 149.

more life – has a workout schedule that combines anaerobic exercise – bodybuilding and aerobic sports – to downhill skiing and cycling.[37] Ray Kurzweil reportedly takes daily "250 supplements, eight to 10 glasses of alkaline water and 10

---

[37] This is the workout schedule of Natasha Vita-More. http://www.natasha.cc/bodybuilder.htm

BODY-PART	EXERCISE	SETS	REPS	WEIGHTS
Delts	Dumbell press - machine	3	8	10, 20, 35
	Dumbell press - free weights	3	8	20,35,25
	Flys - free weights	3	8	10,15,15
	Lateral raises - free weights	3	8	5,10,10
	Chin raises	3 each arm	8	15, 20, 25
Tricepts	Pushdowns - machine	4	8	30,40,70,50
	One arm pushdowns - machine	3 each arm	8	20,40,20
	Reserve pushdown - straight bar	3	8	30,40,30
	Skull crunch - bar	3	8	bar+10,20, 20
	One arm overhead raises - free weights	3 each arm	8	10,17
Back	Lateral pulldowns - machine	4	8	40,60,90,60
	Machine rows - long	4	8	40,70,60
	Machine rows - sit-down	1	15	60
	One arm dumbell rows	3 each arm	8	35, 40
	Bent leg dumbell raises	4	8	15
Abs	Crunches	3	100	

cups of green tea. He also periodically tracks 40 to 50 fitness indicators, down to his 'tactile sensitivity.' Adjustments are made as needed."[38]

BODY PART	EXERCISE	SETS	REPS	WEIGHTS
Biceps	Alternative dumbell curls - free weights	4	8-12	20
	21s	3	7-7-7	15
	or/Barbell bar curls	3	12	30,40,50
	Alternate dumbell crossovers		8	20,20,15
	Concentration curls	3 each arm	8	20
	Reclining dumbell curls	3 each arm	8	15
Thighs/ Quads	Leg extensions	4	8	50,80,110,90
	Leg press	3	8	30,50,90,70
	Angle leg press	4	8	90,180,270, 180
	Hack squat (Smith machine)	3	8	50
	or/Squat (Smith machine)	8	12	50,70,100
Ham- strings/ Glutes	Leg curls	4	8	30,50
	Straight leg dead lifts	4	12	50
	Butt machine	2	15 minutes	advanced
Calves	Seated calf raises	4	30	50
	Hanging leg raises	4	50	
	Machine crunches	2	30	40,60,60

---

[38] Jay Linsay, "Inventor Pursues Immortality," *The Worcester Telegram and Gazette*, 13 February 2005, B5. Ironically this article was on the same page as the obituaries.

Additionally, there are several goals to which one should aspire as the consequence of this dedication to physical fitness, to a transformed body, to a new self. A helpful comparison graph is provided.[39]

What is interesting in this is the utter flexibility of the transhuman, including upgraded genes, gender variability, and heightened intelligence. Also interesting is that the design is impervious to environmental damage. Thus should those not at the transhuman stage continue to muck up the environment, the transhumans need not worry.

---

[39] http://www.natasha.cc/primo3m+comparison.htm

Comparison Chart

20th Century — Body	21st Century — Primo Posthuman
Limited Life span	Ageless
Legacy genes	Replaceable genes
Wears out	Upgrades
Random mistakes	Error correction device
Sense of humanity	Enlightened Transhumanity
Intelligence 100 trillion synapses	Intelligence 100 quadrillion synapses
Single track awareness	Multiple parallel viewpoints
Gender restricted	Gender changeability
Prone to environmental damage	Impervious to environmental damage
Corrosion by irritability, envy, depression	Turbocharged optimism
Elimination messy/gaseous waste	Recycles and purifies waste

And how is such a movement to be started? Typically there is a revolutionary vanguard and the transhumans are no different.

> We call it "The Three Hundred" ... themed from history and limited to that number of participants. These individuals (or organizations) see the potential of the Prize and believe that aging can be defeated. Members of The Three Hundred have made a commitment to creating a better future, one in which the suffering caused by aging is greatly diminished or banished entirely. The unique foresight shared by The Three Hundred at this early stage in aging research will be remembered – they grasped the ring, heard the call and took action when the opportunity first presented itself. The efforts of the Three Hundred will be remembered, like those of their historical counterparts, far into the future.
>
> The Three Hundred is a classical concept, based on a battle that saved the future of Western Civilization: Thermopylae. In 480 B.C., 300 Spartan warriors fought against incredible odds to gain time for the rest of Greece to mobilize against the Persian hordes. Without the delaying action fought at the narrow pass of Thermopylae, the achievements of Greece and our culture as we know it would have been swept away.
>
> The Methuselah Foundation is asking you to follow in the footsteps of this noble Three Hundred, not to risk your lives, but to provide some of your treasure so that we can all live ... and live ... and live. You will help to win time for the human species to beat back an enemy far more dangerous than the ancient Persians: the Grim Reaper himself.
>
> The Three Hundred – a group strictly limited to 300 members – will live on in history, as the Three Hundred of Thermopylae are remembered even to this day. You can be one of them. The names of the 300 Spartans who fought at Thermopylae were engraved

on a stone tablet in Sparta that was still legible seven centuries later. A monument stands to this day to pay homage to their sacrifice. In lending your name to this enterprise, you will be remembered for as long as the human race survives.

The existence of The Three Hundred resonates with those who feel the injustice of the aging process, people who welcome the first serious attempts in human history to fight aging and win. Nine enthusiastic individuals have signed up before we could even make the announcement public. Please visit the following website and read about The Three Hundred:

http://www.mprize.org/index.php?pagename=thethreehundr eddeclaration

What's it worth to you to live 150 healthy years? What's it worth to you to raise the average human lifespan to 150 years, just as a start? These are not idle questions! Membership of The Three Hundred is a meaningful, but affordable commitment: $1,000 a year, by the end of each year, for 25 years. This amounts to $85 a month or $2.75 a day, the equivalent of a visit to Starbucks.

The movement seems to strive for a technical immortality lived out through various forms of virtual reality on the web. Downloading of the self from one computer to another seems to be the transhumanist form of the transmigration of souls, but always in a more perfect form.

FRANCISCAN PERSPECTIVES AND RESPONSES

The move from contemporary genetics and the transhuman movement to a medieval philosophy and theology may seem strange or bizarre to some (or many). Yet I have become convinced that some of the ideas that Bonaventure and Scotus developed in their writings can shed light on some aspects of our contemporary problems. Now since both lived and wrote quite prior to the twenty-first century, it is obvious that neither had knowledge of the theory of evolution, any concept of what sociobiologists refer to as a reproductive strategy, or nanobot technology as a means of having our bodies assume any shape we desire. I am not attempting to bootleg any such theories into their thought. Nor will I use their ideas as a Procrustean bed with which to shape contemporary ideas. Rather, my sense is that Bonaventure and Scotus have some insights that can help clarify the conundrum into which the sociobiologists and transhumanists seem to have gotten themselves.

Scotus and Altruism

I argue that sociobiologists have made a major mistake in their use of the term altruism. My issue is the term, not the behavior – although my concern is not exclusively semantic. That is, while the behaviors described are biologically accurate – in so far as they stick to biology – the significance of these behaviors also has been misinterpreted primarily because of the sociobiologists' almost idiosyncratic use of the term altruism. And it is because of this that they have gotten themselves into what many consider to be a Hobbesian world.

Duns Scotus begins with two distinctions. First is the concept of a nature: a principle of activity by which an entity acts out or actualizes its reality. A being's nature is the reason why an entity acts as it does. Or as he says: "the potency of itself is determined to act, so that so far as itself is concerned, it cannot fail to act when not impeded from without."[40] A nature essentially explains why an entity acts as it does.

A will, on the other hand, "is not of itself so determined, but can perform either this act or its opposite, or can either act or not act at all."[41] Thus, the reason why this act was done as opposed to another is that the will is the will and

---

[40] *Quaestiones in Metaphysicam* 1, q. 15, A. 2. Quoted in Allan B. Wolter, O.F.M., *Duns Scotus on the Will and Morality* (Washington: Catholic University of America, 1986), 151.

[41] Wolter, *Duns Scotus on the Will and Morality*.

can elicit an act in opposite ways. Following Anselm, Scotus distinguishes two movements in the will as the *affectio commodi* – the inclination to seek what is advantageous or good for one's self – and the *affectio justitiae* – the inclination to seek the good in itself.

In this section I focus on the *affectio commodi,* the will to do what is to our advantage, perfection or welfare. This affection or inclination is a nature seeking its own fulfillment. For Scotus, this *affectio commodi* is not an elicited act. Rather it is a natural appetite necessarily seeking its own perfection. As Scotus says:

> That it does so *necessarily* is obvious, because a nature could not remain a nature without being inclined to its own perfection. Take away this inclination and you destroy the nature. But this natural appetite is nothing other than an inclination of this sort to its proper perfection; therefore the will as nature necessarily wills its perfection, which consists above all in happiness, and it desires such by its natural appetite.[42]

Allan B. Wolter provides an interesting commentary on this concept:

> ... all striving, all activity stems from an imperfection in the agent. As the etymological derivation of the word itself suggests, nature [from *nascor*, to be born] is literally what a thing was born to be, or more precisely, born to become, for nature as an active agent is essentially dynamic in a Faustian sense. It is restless until it achieves self-perfection. Since what perfects a thing is its good and since this striving for what is good is a form of love, we could say with Socrates that all activity is sparked by love.[43]

---

[42] *Ordinatio* IV, suppl. dist, 49, qq. 9-10. In Wolter, *Duns Scotus on the Will and Morality*, 185.

[43] Allan B. Wolter, O.F.M. "Native Freedom of the Will as a Key to the Ethics of Scotus," in *The Philosophical Theology Of John Duns Scotus*, ed. Marilyn McCord Adams (Ithaca, NY: Cornell University Press, 1990), 150.

This love, however, is neither objective nor directed to the good of another, regardless of whether or not this other being might be a kin. It is self-centered and directed to seeking its own welfare. As Wolter further comments,

> If at times we encounter what seems to be altruistic behavior in the animal world, or instance, it is always a case where the "nature" or "species" is favored at the expense of the individual. But nature, either in its individual concretization or as a self-perpetuating species, must of necessity seek its own perfection. Such is its supreme value and the ultimate goal of all its loves.[44]

As Wolter interprets Scotus here, when an individual entity or a nature acts, it seeks its own good or what is to its advantage. This is not cause for surprise for this is what a nature does, whether looked at as an individual representative of the species or as the species as a whole. The *affectio commodi* drives the being "to seek his perfection and happiness in all he does."[45]

What is significant about this perspective – particularly in the context of the sociobiologists – is that for Scotus, and indeed for the entire classical philosophical tradition from Plato forward, seeking one's own perfection is a good. It is "not some evil to be eradicated. For it too represents a God-given drive implanted in man's rational nature which leads him to seek his true happiness ..."[46] In fact, to ignore our perfection or to give it no standing in our actions is an act of injustice to one's self.

I argue that what Wilson and Dawkins refer to as genetic selfishness is what Scotus refers to as the *affectio commodi*. The significance of the Scotistic position is, on the one hand,

---

[44] Wolter, "Native Freedom of the Will," 150.
[45] Wolter, "Native Freedom of the Will," 151.
[46] Wolter, "Native Freedom of the Will," 151.

that he too sees the same kind of tendency present in human nature as do the sociobiologists but, on the other hand, he, together with the entire philosophical tradition to that time, sees that behavior as a good because it achieves the perfection of the individual and the species. That is, for Scotus, the *affectio commodi* is that dimension of human nature that leads us to seek our fulfillment or perfection as a human. This affection is a good precisely because it leads to our perfection.

There is, however, a critical difference between Scotus and the sociobiologists. For the sociobiologists, the behavior comes from evolutionary success whereas for Scotus the cause is the creative will of God expressed in creation. Nonetheless, though the origin is quite different, the behavior is the same. Part of the difference surely lies in both philosophical and theological frameworks. But another part of the difference lies in that Scotus sees self-perfecting behavior as a good while the sociobiologists describe this as selfish – which even in their framework has a negative connotation.

But there remains this issue raised by the sociobiologists: is such genetically selfish activity the only possible mode of human activity? Or as Scotus would phrase it, can we see and actualize a good beyond ourselves and our perfection, beyond the *affectio commodi*? Scotistic thought would agree with the sociobiologists that as natures we, like any other nature, seek our good and our individual perfection and that we do so necessarily. But it would disagree that this is selfish in the pejorative sense of sociobiology. In fact, I think from a Scotistic perspective, the sociobiologists discussion of genetic selfishness makes no sense at all and is a significant distortion of human existence as the next section will argue.

Scotus calls the *affectio justitiae* or the affection for justice the source of true freedom or liberty of the will and is the basis for his claim that true freedom goes beyond freedom understood as choice. Additionally, the *affectio justitiae is* the means by which we can transcend nature and go beyond our individually defined good and ourselves to see the value of another being.

Scotus's affirmation here is that we have the capacity to value an entity for its own sake, independent of its personal or social utility. As Scotus would phrase it, we have the ability to transcend the capacity to do justice to ourselves by doing justice to the good itself. The strong claim is that we are capable of recognizing goods distinct from our self-perfection and independent of our interests and choosing them even though such a choice may run counter to our personal self-interest or what does justice to my own nature.

> The will by freely moderating these natural and necessary tendencies to happiness and self-perfection is able to transcend its nature and choose Being and Goodness for their own sake.... Thus the free will is not confined to objects or goods that perfect self, but is capable of an act of love.... love is the most free of all acts and the one that most perfectly expresses the will's freedom to determine itself as it pleases.[47]

The conclusion is that one can distinguish at least a good and a better in human life. What is good in human life is a life that perfects us, that brings our being to a greater actualization. This is the realization of the *affectio commodi* but it is a realization of the good for one's self. John Boler states this bluntly: "morality cannot be an extension or refinement of a project of self-realization and/or eudaimonism (as that Aristotelian theme had been developed in the Middle Ages) but requires precisely going beyond it."[48] What is better is the transcendence of self either to appreciate goods independent of us or even to curb our legitimate interest in self-perfection to seek the good of others for their own sakes. This is the realization of the *affectio justitiae*.

---

[47] Valerius Messerich, O.F.M., "The Awareness of Causal Initiative and Existential Responsibility in the Thought of Duns Scotus," in *De Doctrina Ioannis Duns Scoti* 2: *Problemata Philosophica* (Rome: Acta Congressus Scotistici Internat., 1968), 629-44, at 630-31.

[48] John Boler, "Transcending the Natural: Duns Scotus on the Two Affections of the Will" in *American Catholic Philosophical Quarterly*, LXVII (1993): 109-126, at 110.

Guided by the *affectio commodi*, the agent will seek the fulfillment of its nature and in doing so will achieve happiness, it will achieve the fulfillment of its nature. It will act in a way "continuous with the broad area of appetitive behavior throughout nature."[49] All well and good, except that on this account the agent is not free, is not acting voluntarily; the agent is necessarily acting according to its nature. A free act, one distinguished from one of the agent's nature, requires "the fact that antecedent (natural) conditions do not determine the self-movement of the will."[50] The payoff of this analysis is that as free agents, we can act beyond nature, even beyond one's own nature. As Boler observes "Scotus seems to be appealing to the idea that, in the very making of certain choices, we can realize that it is open to us to act in a different way."[51]

Self-realization or self-actualization programs seem to be limited to what Scotus calls the *affectio commodi*—the realization of one's nature, the actualization of one's potential – in the better programs – as a rational agent. The problem with such an argument is not simply that morality or happiness is reduced to the good for one's self, though that is a problem, but rather that this schema, the traditional Aristotelian and eudaimonistic one, is that "a rational nature is simply a higher form of a natural agent...."[52] The problem is that this simply sells the human agent short because the human on this account acts according to his or her nature and in doing this acts necessary, not freely and thus not morally. "Being moral cannot be analyzed in terms of an agent's nature because being free is precisely not being 'in' a nature."[53] For Scotus the *affectio justitiae* grounds the capacity for morality precisely in that this affection for justice can moderate the *affectio commodi*, can transcend the happiness presented

---

[49] Boler, "Transcending the Natural," 116.

[50] Boler, "Transcending the Natural," 115.

[51] Boler, "Transcending the Natural," 118.

[52] Boler, "Transcending the Natural," 122.

[53] John Boler, "The Moral Psychology of Duns Scotus: some Preliminary Questions," 38.

to it by its nature and its natural inclinations, and can in fact act beyond its nature. Such is the reality of freedom and the basis of morality. It is not sufficient for us to know what is possible, to know what will satisfy us, to know what will fulfill our nature. The foundation of morality is the capacity for transcending our nature and moral actions are those that take priority over self-realization.

Put existentially:

A free choice, then is the meaning of existence and the total initiative is left to man to rightly moderate his natural tendencies in the pursuit of being for its own sake. And in this sense one's existence is one's own responsibility and depends on one's causal initiative as an ultimate response to Being or Nothingness.[54]

Put ethically:

right reason also recognizes that our self-perfection, even through union with God in love, is not of supreme value. It enables man, in short, to recognize that the drive for self-perfection paradoxically must not go unbridled if it is to achieve its goal, but must be channeled lest it destroy the harmony of the universe intended by God.[55]

What is most helpful about this perspective is that while it affirms self-perfection, ultimately such perfection is not an end in itself. To "be all that we can be" we must step beyond the confines of self and actualize that most free of all acts, an act of love. For only then do we find ourselves open to the depths of reality. And in the steadfast adherence to that beloved, we realize the fullness of freedom. And this vision stands in strong contrast to the transhumanist movement that seeks to develop the self only, to seek self-perfection as

---

[54] Messerich, "The Awareness of Causal Initiative," 631.
[55] Messerich, "The Awareness of Causal Initiative," 631.

an end in itself, and to free oneself from the shackles of finite, material creation. Bonaventure, in contrast, finds the meaning and purpose of humanity precisely imbedded in the deepest meaning of created reality.

Bonaventure and the Fully Human

When we use the phrase "I'm in the middle of a project" or words to that effect, we generally connote that we are quite busy. Sometimes the phrase, given a particular hostile inflection, suggests that we are about to be overtaken by events and that we want to escape this middle as soon as possible. Between the rock and the hard place is not a position of comfort. We also use the term of the middle to describe someone who either has not or cannot make a decision. We all know people who perpetually seem to be in the middle – "on the fence," we say. And the middle frequently suggests a compromise position, again a stance that has negative undertones. In all these instances the phrase "the middle" has a negative connotation. It indicates a place from which we want to escape either because of the chaos there or because it suggests a compromised position.

Yet it is this middle position that Bonaventure has defined as the ground of human dignity. As Schaeffer says, "The central idea of the present study [which] finds its best and shortest expression in the formula *homo in medio constitutus* – 'man is placed at the center.'"[56] This formula both locates the position of humans within the world and also gives the metaphysical grounding to their status and role. We now turn to Bonaventure's positive account of what it means to be "in the middle," a position that contrasts greatly with the transhumanist position of getting out of the middle of things into individual bliss.

God as the creator and the fountain-fullness of all is revealed in the creation of the multiplicity of entities and in

---

[56] Alexander Schaeffer, O.F.M., "The Position and Function of Man in the Created World According to St. Bonaventure," *Franciscan Studies* 20 (1960): 261-316, 279.

the order that exists in creation. For Bonaventure, such an order is structural:

> The most perfect form of creation is not a world in which every being is equally perfect; it is the present order with its harmonious gradation, because it is in this condition the best manifestation of the divine power, wisdom, and goodness of the Creator. [57]

Such an order reflects the very image of the Trinity by manifesting God's power, wisdom, and goodness.

Creation manifests the *power* of God by revealing the greatness of extension, i.e., in the quantity and variety of creatures as well as in the creation of beings with opposite natures. A particular dimension of God's power is that it not only unites extremes – matter and spirit – but also creates a union between them.

Creation manifests the *wisdom* of God by manifesting a sufficient order; Bonaventure states this as follows:

> But the wisdom of an artist is manifested in the perfection of *order,* and every order necessarily has a *lowest* level, a *highest* level, and an *intermediate* level. If therefore, the lowest level is the purely *corporeal* nature, the highest level the *spiritual* nature, and the intermediate level is *composed of both,* then the wisdom of God would not be shown *perfectly* unless [God] had made *all these levels.* [58]

God's goodness is manifest through diffusion and communication of itself to another. This is, on the one hand, another demonstration of the powerful first principle that Bonaventure evokes so frequently: *"bonum est diffusivum sui."* On the other hand, this diffusion of goodness is specified through an act of communication. While the act of creation communicates life and the capacity to know, Bonaventure states a more specific form of communication: "This more im-

---

[57] Schaeffer, "The Position and Function of Man," 293.
[58] *II Sent.* 1, 2, i, 2; fund. 2; quoted in Schaeffer, 1960, 298.

mediate and perfect manifestation consists in a reproduction and *dramatic presentation of the act of communication itself* somewhere in creation."[59]

The human is the locus of the critical act of communication and reveals the human as both the completion and consummation of God's work of creation: situated as the critical link that unites the two extremes of creation. And Bonaventure sees in the human both the completion and consummation of God's work of creation.

> Because the first principle was most powerful, wise, and good in production, and because [God] has made this manifest in all his effects in a certain way, he ought to manifest this most impressively in his last and most noble effect. Such is man, whom he produced last among all creatures so that in man he should appear most potently, and the accomplishment of the divine works should be reflected in him.[60]

All of creation, which manifests the divine goodness by virtue of its existence and destiny, is ordained to God as its final end, and is to participate in God's glory at the end of time. All of created reality is equal with respect to this. But Bonaventure makes a distinction with respect to how creatures participate in this divine goodness: there is immediate participation with the spiritual beings and mediate participation with the material world.[61] This mode of participation is either because by their nature they are made to participate as are the angels or because by their nature they serve those who participate as do the animals and the rest of inanimate creation.

These distinctions lead Bonaventure to the conclusion that the human, because of the status of being constituted in the middle, functions as "the mediator between the corporeal creatures and God who alone is the ultimate end of all

---

[59] *II Sent.* 1, 2, i, 2; fund. 2; quoted in Schaeffer, 1960, 309.
[60] *Breviloquium*, II, 10.
[61] Schaeffer, (1960), 312.

things."[62] This leads to a twofold vocation: the human is the highest creature to whom all of creation is directed and is the one through whom creation receives its full participation in the kingdom of God.

Bonaventure's position is that all of created reality is directed to humankind. On this basis he describes humans as monarchs of the visible universe because the creature which reconciles the greatest extremes in itself most perfectly manifests the power, wisdom, and goodness of God and because of his doctrine of the plurality of corporeal forms in material creatures, which says that each form is "essentially ordained towards the next higher one."[63]

Thus Bonaventure can say:

All desire of sensitive and corporeal nature is designed and intended so that the soul, a form existing, living, sentient, and intelligent, as if in the mode of an intelligent orbit, leads back to its beginning in which it is perfected and beatified.

And because through its origin the soul tends toward freedom of choice, it excels in this regard all corporeal power by its very freedom of choice. Through this all things are born to serve it, and nothing can rule it except God alone, not fate nor the power of the star's position.

Wherefore it is unquestionably true that we are 'the end of all things which exist,' and all corporeal matter was made for human service so that by all these things humankind may ascent to loving and praising the Creator of the universe, whose providence disposes of all.[64]

---

[62] Schaeffer, (1960), 313.

[63] Alexander Schaeffer, O.F.M., "The Position and Function of Man in the Created World According to St. Bonaventure," *Franciscan Studies* 21 (1961): 230-382.

[64] *Breviloquium*, 2, 3-5.

Thus the material universe reaches its fulfillment in humanity and humanity reaches its fulfillment in God. Through this mediating act of humans, therefore, the material world reaches and will ultimately be transformed by the glory of God. In reaching its final end of union with God, humankind, through its bodily dimension, brings created reality to participation in the glory of God.

Although the image of God in humans ordains them to God, gives them the capacity of entering a relation with God, and enables them to achieve beatification in God, the realization of the possibility is impossible without God's direct intervention. Although the image of God imprinted in humankind gives us the natural disposition for such a reality, the actualization awaits the initiative of God.

The actualization constitutes the closing of the circle opened at creation and now closed through redemption. The first phase of this, according to Schaeffer, is the formation of the supernatural image in humans. This is accomplished through the infusion of sanctifying grace, which elevates the soul and develops a supernatural structure of virtues within the individual person. The second phase is the transformation of the three distinct structural elements of the image of God in humans by sanctifying grace: intellect, memory, and will. Thus is the person in his or her entirety totally transformed through grace so that the image of God within each shines forth again.

This transformation continues at the end of life, where one finds one's ultimate fulfillment in what Bonaventure calls *deiformitas:* an infusion of sanctifying grace that disposes one to find total fulfillment in the continuous act of loving God.

Hence in man's reward that godliness of glory *(deiformitas)* is given him by which he is conformed to God, sees *God* clearly with his reason, loves *God* fully with his will, and retains him forever in his memory. Thus the whole soul lives, the whole soul is richly endowed in its three powers, the whole soul is joined to God, is united to him and rests in him, finding in him all good, peace, light, and eternal sufficiency. Hence, situated "in the state of all good in a perfect gathering" and achieving eternal life, man is said to be happy and glorious.[65]

Finally, the full reality of redemption and the restoration of humankind to its original place in God's plan require the resurrection of the body and its reunion with the soul. One reason for this is that it is not souls that are redeemed but the person who is composed of both. For the soul "has a tendency naturally implanted to rejoin the body"[66] and in the union of body and soul, "the desire of matter for higher forms comes to rest."[67] Thus final perfection is achieved in the reunion of the soul and body.

The other consequence of this is that through the resurrection of the body and its participation in the restoration of all in God, the whole of creation too can participate in this final glorification. Just as through the sin of the first humans the world was subjected to disorder, so now in the restoration of original justice in humans the world too is set right once again. Because the human body is composed of the elements of the world, the cosmos finds its representation before the throne of God. And though the world of plants and animals will pass away because its function is fulfilled because humans can now see God directly instead of indirectly through the exemplars and vestiges of the created world-plants and animals also participate in the final glory through humankind, which bears a likeness to every creature. Since humans are "the focal point in the order of creation ... [their] ... redemption and beatification restore and perfect this order and bring it to a final completion."[68]

> Finally, because the world ought to be consumed when man faces consummation, and man is to be consumed when the number of the elect in glory shall be complete and all tend to this state as their ultimate and

---

[65] *Breviloquium*, 7, 3.

[66] *Breviloquium*, 7, 4.

[67] Schaeffer, "The Position and Function of Man," (1961), 375.

[68] Schaeffer, "The Position and Function of Man," (1961), 380.

complete end, it follows that upon the completion of that process there must be an end to the motion of celestial nature and quiet in it, and likewise elemental transmutations must cease and consequently generation both animal and vegetative must cease. Since all these matters are subordinated to the most noble form, which is the rational soul, hence, by virtue of its place among spirits, its status and complement must be established in other precedents. Hence the celestial bodies in a quiet and a fullness of light are said to be rewarded. The elements which no longer have the power of multiplying by a mutual transmutation are said to perish not alone as regards their substance but as regards their mutual activity and passivity, and most especially as regards their active qualities. Things vegetative and things sensitive, since they do not possess the power of perpetual life and eternal duration, for such is the degree of their nobility, must be consumed in their own natures and yet in such a way that they are saved in their principles and somehow in likeness, namely, in man who has a likeness to every kind of creature. Hence in man's renovation and glorification we can speak of the renovation of all and in some fashion of the reward of all.[69]

Bonaventure grounds human dignity in terms of the location of humans within the created order and our function within that order. For Bonaventure, this meant that humans, who were created last, according to the biblical narrative, are highest in the order of creation and that the function of humans is to be mediators by representing the world before God and ensuring the participation of all of reality in redemption. Finally, our dignity consists in the capacity for *deiformitas,* the infusion of grace that totally transforms and restores the tarnished image of God in humans and leads to the total fulfillment of the human in a continuous act of loving God.

---

[69] *Breviloquium,* 7,4,7.

This vision of human dignity allows Bonaventure: to affirm humans, but not at the expense of nature; to articulate a vocation for humans, but one inclusive of creation; to provide a positive relation between humans and nature, which can ground an ecological ethic. For Bonaventure, such a position is not a claim to power. Rather it is a position of service: to God, to one's neighbor, and to nature. Position, for Bonaventure, does not confer power – it calls to service.

One of the significant dimensions of Bonaventure's thought is the place of nature in his overall scheme. Nature is a locus of revelation, a book given us by the graciousness of the Creator that we might learn of the Creator. The ground of this is the doctrine of exemplarism through which Bonaventure argues that what is created bears the likeness of its Maker and provides a way of understanding qualities of this Maker. Because the Creator has left personal traces in what has been made, we can work our way back to an understanding of who this Creator is.

Second, nature is the means through which the incarnation becomes possible. There are two reasons for this. First, matter is prerequisite of human existence. Second, the reconciliation of opposites shows the greatest wisdom and in the incarnation we have the reconciliation of infinite and finite, spirit and matter, divinity and humanity. Matter has a value beyond the instrumental for it is taken up into a most intimate relation with the Divinity itself.

Third, humans are embedded in nature as deeply as any other created entity. Indeed, we are animated flesh. Through our bodiliness we participate in the mineral world and the animal world. Although Bonaventure predates the theory of evolution, this theory captures a real sense of the continuity of humans with nature.

For Bonaventure, such continuity is not a random or chance event. Our materiality looks beyond itself. It is transformed through the form so that the form of an entity both gives it its perfection and prepares it for the next higher form. The matter of our reality is not left behind or rejected as we develop. We do not have a Cartesian dichotomization of mind and machine, but rather the bringing of matter into the heart of reality.

Bonaventure's vision of the human vocation can be found in his understanding of Francis, who so submitted to the presence of grace in his life that it completely filled and shaped him. Thus in the life of Francis we can see a restoration of the original relation between God and humans, and between humans and nature.

Bonaventure alludes to two events that demonstrate this. First is the taming of the wolf and the calming of storms at Gubbio. Francis said that if people repented and remained faithful to God, these plagues of nature would cease. And so they did. Second is the cauterizing of Francis's eyes to relieve the pain. Francis made the sign of the cross over the hot iron and prayed, and then it was applied. Afterward Francis reported that he felt neither heat nor pain. Bonaventure provides the theological interpretation:

> The man of God had attained to such a degree of purity that his flesh was subject to his spirit, and his spirit to God in a wonderful harmony and agreement, and all creatures were thus in marvelous subjection to his will and command, who was himself the faithful servant of the Creator.[70]

Thus as we actualize our redemption initiated at baptism, we enter more and more into the order intended by God. As we do this, we begin to actualize this reality in our own lives. This will evoke a response of respect and reverence to nature, not one of dominance and dominion. Stewardship is actualized not by lording it over creation but by appreciating the goodness of nature and by being its voice before God.

The critical difference between Bonaventure and the ecological ethic so prevalent in the West today is that Bonaventure presents an ethic of restoration and responsibility as opposed to the traditional ethic of dominance and exploita-

---

[70] Schaeffer, "The Position and Function of Man," (1961), 327.

tion. In the Bonaventurian vision, the shift to dominance was one of the fruits of sin that brought about a distorted relation with animals. First, the clouding of vision by sin prevented us from seeing clearly how animals reflected the beauty of God in their existence and diversity. Second, animals were no longer to serve human needs or, if wild, to be a punishment for sin and an opportunity to learn patience. Sin disrupted not only the relation between God and humankind, but also the order within nature itself.

Although redemption has repaired the broken relation between God and humanity, the effects of sin remain and affect our daily lives. However, as Schaeffer summarizes Bonaventure, "The more the re-formation of man progresses and approaches the state of original innocence, so much the more is also restored the original relationship of the animals and other creatures to man."[71]

CONCLUDING PERSPECTIVES

The perspectives on human nature that the Franciscan tradition offers is a profound challenge to our contemporary American way of life and the visions proposed by some proponents of a narrow view of genetics and a radically individualistic view of humans.

First, it is a challenge to the way we act with respect to nature. This caution is not based on an order of nature deemed to be inviolate or normative for human action. Rather it is a caution that recognizes that what we see is not the totality of reality. Bonaventure's vision is that the whole is greater than the sum of the parts. This is an argument against reductionism, but it is also an affirmation of the profound potentialities of matter. Recall Bonaventure's position on seminal reasons: "There are in matter the germs of forms upon which the action which is to develop them will operate.... Matter was cre-

---

[71] Schaeffer, "The Position and Function of Man," (1961), 326.

ated pregnant with a something from which the agent draws out the form."[72]

Louis Mackey captures a different dimension of this in discussing the limits of the epistemological theories of realism and nominalism:

> The realist, who demeans singulars in what he takes to be the interest of universals, and the nominalist, who consigns universals to oblivion to save the honor of the singular both commit fallacies of the misplaced concreteness. St. Bonaventure would have said that both realist and nominalist err by mistaking the present scene – creatures in isolation from God – for the whole show. They regard creatures as things-in-themselves (which they are not) instead of seeing them as signs and expressions of the eternal art (which they are).[73]

To see the present scene as the whole show or to mistake what is for what might be is to miss, as Hopkins phrases it, "the dearest freshness deep down things." Such a perspective does not prohibit interventions in nature. Rather it cautions us that such interventions go beyond what is seen or what can be modeled even through the most sophisticated imaging technologies. Such interventions touch but a part of what reality is and to miss that is to miss the potential of reality. Such a recognition of the potentials of nature and our embeddedness within it can lead to a continuous conversion of heart so that we can once again "read the Book of Creation, [to] receive the full service of things below him, and to be in this way their decisive mediator on the way to God."[74]

Second, the Franciscan vision is a challenge to how we view ourselves and others. Our dignity comes from being an

---

[72] Etienne Gilson, *The Philosophy of St. Bonaventure*, translated by Illtyd Trethowan (Patterson, NJ: St. Anthony Guild Press, 1965), 269.

[73] Louis Mackey, "Singular and Universal: A Franciscan Perspective," *Franciscan Studies* 39 (1979): 130-50, 140.

[74] Schaeffer, "The Position and Function of Man," (1961), 332.

image of God. For Bonaventure this consists in our having been created in the image of the Trinity with mind, knowledge, and love. As created this means that

> man is right when his intelligence coincides with the supreme truth in knowing, [when] his will conforms to the supreme loving, and [when] his power is united to the supreme power in acting. Now this is when man is turned to God in his total self.[75]

However, we know that we are not fully turned to God. Although we have turned from God, we retain the image and still desire this totality of Goodness. This image is restored through the redemptive work of Christ: "As Incarnate Word, Christ reestablishes man as Trinitarian image and with the Spirit brings him back to the unity of the Father."[76] Thus at the most profound level of our being we are shaped by the hand of the Creator and reflect the innermost dynamism of the Trinity.

This perspective can serve as the basis for a transformation in how we view ourselves and others. Although we were created in the image of God, we fell from grace and are in the process of conversion so that this image can once again appear within us and transform our lives. This is true of each of us and is the basis for, first, understanding why we act as we do, and second, what we can expect of each other. We act as we do because the process of transformation is not complete within us. Thus we forget our true vocation of service to others and creation. Yet we may expect the best because of our vocation to *deiformitas*.

Third, our dignity is not a prize or something to be clung to. It is a vocation. And the vocation consists in our being the voice of creation. Because of our being created "in the middle," we stand in a unique place and participate in both the spiritual and material dimensions of creation. The monarchi-

---

[75] *II Sentences*, proem, in Ewert Cousins, *Bonaventure and the Coincidence of Opposites* (Chicago: Franciscan Herald Press, 1977), 130.

[76] Cousins, *Bonaventure and the Coincidence of Opposites*, 130.

cal status that Bonaventure bestows on us and his statement that we are the apex of the material world is not a claim of human pride gone wild. It is not the basis for power or dominion over creation. It is, rather, an accurate metaphysical description of where Bonaventure sees us located within the world of creation.

The vocation of monarchy is exercised through our freedom in which we recognize our ordination to God. Thus the order intended by God is realized: the world, which was made for us, serves us and we in turn serve the One who made the heavens and the earth – and humanity as well.[77] Such a vocation is captured well in the words of Teilhard de Chardin:

> May the might of those invincible hands direct and transfigure for the great world you have in mind that earthly travail which I have gathered into my heart and now offer in its entirety. Remold it, rectify it, recast it down to the depths from whence it springs. You know how your creatures can come into being only, like shoot from stem, as part of an endlessly renewed process of evolution.
>
> Do you now therefore, speaking through my lips, pronounce over this earthly travail your twofold efficacious word: the word without which all that our wisdom and our experience have built up must totter and crumble – the word through which all our most far-reaching speculations and our encounter with the universe are come together into a unity. Over every living thing which is to spring up, to grow, to flower, to ripen during this day, say again the words: This is my Body. And over every death-force which waits in readiness to corrode, to wither, to cut down, speak again your commanding words which express the supreme mystery of faith: This is my Blood.[78]

---

[77] Schaeffer, "The Position and Function of Man," (1961), 323.

[78] Pierre Teilhard de Chardin, S.J., "Mass Over the World," In *Hymn of the Universe* (NY: Harper and Row, 1961), 22-23.

Or, as DeBenedictis expresses it: "Thus, having been placed in a world pregnant with the divine imprint, man has been assigned the role of leading the world back to its Author by seeing him, praising him, and loving him in all things."[79] Thus, rather than seeking to have our particular genetic profile replicated as much as possible or to escape our finiteness or our limitations, the Franciscan tradition invites us to a vision of communal graciousness in which we celebrate the particular and unique beauty of each individual in all of creation. Instead of seeking either to succumb to nature or to get out of nature, the wisdom of both Scotus and Bonaventure asks us to both recognize the role of freedom within nature and also to celebrate the realities of nature's full potentials. The Franciscan tradition asks us to appreciate that in this created and finite world we have the vocation of participating in the transformation of the world and, by speaking on behalf of all creation, being its mediator by joining its word of cosmic praise to that of the risen and transformed Christ.

---

[79] Matthew DeBenedictis, O.F.M., *The Social Thought of Saint Bonaventure* (Washington, DC: The Catholic University of America Press, 1946), 44.

Virtues and Vices: A Franciscan Approach

Kathryn Getek

I begin in gratitude to Sister Indefinite Article; this is a Franciscan perspective on virtues and vices. Therefore, it is merely one possible intersection between the tradition of virtue, which stretches back far beyond even the earliest Christian sources, and the inspired tradition that emerged out of the lives of a few men and women amidst the Assisi hills at the turn of the thirteenth century. Virtue ethics, the former of these two, is a moral method with multiple points of entry. Here, I am most interested in placing a Franciscan approach in conversation with the virtue tradition as it has developed upon the foundations of Aristotle and Thomas Aquinas. Virtue takes up an "ethics of being" in addition to an "ethics of doing." The moral starting point is found in the questions of *Who am I? Who ought I to become? How ought I to get there?*[1] The crucial building blocks of our moral lives are not limited to discrete actions which may be right or wrong, but also include our habits and dispositions which we might describe as good or bad. Of course, action and disposition are interrelated; a good person will seek to do the right action. Virtue ethics calls our attention to the cultivation of habits as a central practice of moral development. As will be clear, virtues and vices were significant elements in the theological landscape

---

[1] See Alasdair MacIntyre, *After Virtue: A Study in Moral Theory* (Notre Dame, IN: University of Notre Dame, 1981).

of Francis and his successors. In fact, I attempt to develop some guideposts for a distinctively Franciscan virtue ethic.

This paper proceeds in three main sections. First, I examine works of two Franciscan writers: St. Bonaventure, thirteenth century theologian, philosopher, and minister general of the Franciscan order; and John of Caulibus, fourteenth century friar and preacher. With a focus on the latter, I explore Franciscan virtues and vices based on the exemplary virtue of Christ. Second, I consider the relationship between these and the traditional cardinal virtues, suggesting a series of correspondences between the two and considering the role of the Aristotelian mean. Third and finally, I examine the end of Franciscan virtue and conclude with four points of reflection to develop the key moral contributions of a Franciscan approach to virtues and vices.

I. BONAVENTURE AND CAULIBUS ON THE VIRTUES OF CHRIST

CHRISTOLOGICAL VS. ANTHROPOLOGICAL VIRTUE

If we were to take up a definite article and search for the Franciscan virtues, the difficulty of the quest would be immediately obvious. A website for Australian vocations to the Order of Friars Minor speaks of the Franciscan virtues of peace, joy, and compassion.[2] Franciscan Penance in the Confraternity of Penitents names poverty, humility, littleness, love, simplicity, faith, self-sacrifice, and peace.[3] The vaults of the Lower Basilica of San Francesco illustrate the virtues of obedience, chastity, poverty, prudence, and humility. The appearance of Francis as a model for Dante in *The Divine Com-*

---

[2] National Vocations Directory, "Franciscan Friars – OFM;"http://www. catholicozvocations.org.au/directory/religious/franciscan_friars.html; Internet, accessed February 20, 2008.

[3] Franciscan Penance in the Confraternity of Penitents; http://www. penitents.org/franciscanpenance.htm; Internet, accessed February 20, 2008.

edy features the two virtues of poverty and humility.[4] The multiple permutations of Franciscan virtue witness to the fact that there is likely no criteria by which we can identify *the* comprehensive and definitive set of Franciscan virtues. I propose, however, that there is good reason for this. While the Thomistic synthesis treats virtue according to a well-ordered anthropology of human powers and appetites,[5] Franciscan virtue instead relies most fundamentally on Christology. In Christ, there is endless virtue and goodness rather than a discrete system of human powers to be perfected. Thus, we find no clear delimitation or sufficient structure by which we can definitively identify Franciscan virtues. I contend that Franciscan virtue and vice are not only derived from Christology but from a characteristically Franciscan interpretation of the Incarnation of Christ and Christ's work of salvation. It is an interpretation grounded in the suffering of Christ, the one who "made himself poor in this world"[6] and "Who bore the suffering of the cross to save His sheep."[7] To explore this Christological virtue of the Franciscan tradition, I briefly consider the work of Saint Bonaventure followed by a text of meditations from fourteenth century Franciscan friar, John of Caulibus.

---

[4] Ronald Herzman, "From Francis to Solomon: Eschatology in the Sun," in *Dante for the New Millennium*, ed. Teodolinda Barolini and H. Wayne Storey (New York: Fordham University Press, 2003), 323.

[5] For Aquinas, the cardinal virtues are each assigned to a particular power or appetite as the subject of the virtue: prudence perfects practical reason, justice perfects the will or intellectual appetite, temperance perfects the concupiscible appetite, and fortitude perfects the irascible appetite. Similar correspondences are made for the theological virtues: the subject of faith is the intellect while hope and charity reside in the will.

[6] Francis of Assisi, *The Later Rule*, Ch. VI, in *Francis of Assisi: Early Documents*, Vols. 1-2, *The Saint*, ed. Regis J. Armstrong, J.A. Wayne Hellmann, and William J. Short (New York: New City Press, 1999-2000), 103.

[7] Francis of Assisi, *The Admonitions*, Ch. VI, in *FA:ED* 1, 131.

BONAVENTURE ON CHRISTOLOGICAL VIRTUES
AND EXEMPLARY VIRTUES

Christ lies at the center of St. Bonaventure's theology. In the Prologue of the *Breviloquium* we learn that theology is akin to a ladder with its feet on the earth, taking the necessary knowledge from natural things, and stretching to the top reaches of heaven. In this way, theology is modeled after Christ who links human and divine nature and is the middle person of the Trinity.[8] As the "exemplary of all things," Christ manifests true virtue in his incarnation: "the Son of God, the very small and poor and humble One ... made of earth."[9] In addition, our salvation is accomplished by the exemplary virtue of Christ in the "the humility of the cross."[10] Bonaventure explains how Christ restored humanity through his all-efficacious example that reveals the way to "the summit of virtue." He reasons that nothing could show humans "the way to virtue more clearly than the example of a death endured for the sake of divine justice and obedience...."[11] Bonaventure finds the ethical center of Christ in the event of the ascension and so, like Christ, "the Christian must rise *from strength to strength*, and not stand still at the terminal point of virtue, for by so doing he would cease to be virtuous."[12]

Poverty and humility are two of the primary virtues that Bonaventure finds in the cross of Christ.[13] These two virtues receive particular emphasis in the image of Christ depicted

---

[8] John F. Quinn, "The Moral Philosophy of St. Bonaventure," in *Bonaventure and Aquinas: Enduring Philosophers* (Norman, OK: University of Oklahoma Press, 1976), 26; see Bonaventure, *The Works of Bonaventure: Cardinal, Seraphic Doctor, and Saint*, Vol. II, *The Breviloquium*, trans. José de Vinck (Paterson, NJ: St. Anthony Guild Press, 1963), Prologue 3.2., 13.

[9] Bonaventure, *The Works of Bonaventure: Cardinal, Seraphic Doctor, and Saint*, Vol. V, *The Collations on the Six Days*, trans. José de Vinck (Paterson, NJ: St. Anthony Guild Press, 1970), 1.22, 12.

[10] *The Collations on the Six Days*, 1.23, 12-13.

[11] *The Breviloquium*, IV, Ch. 9.2, 170-71.

[12] *The Collations on the Six Days*, 1.32, 16.

[13] Elizabeth A. Dreyer, "A Condescending God: Bonaventure's Theology of the Cross," in *The Cross in Christian Tradition: From Paul to Bonaventure* (New York: Paulist Press, 2000), 199.

in Bonaventure's *Disputed Questions on Evangelical Perfec-*
tion and in the *Defense of the Mendicants.*[14] To consider poverty and humility, among other virtues, I turn now to another
Franciscan rendering of the example of Christ, one which is
explicitly aimed toward the cultivation of virtue.

Caulibus on Christological virtues

The *Meditations on the Life of Christ* is among the most
popular and influential Franciscan works of the fourteenth
century. Although originally attributed to Bonaventure, its
author has been recognized, since the end of the eighteenth
century, as John of Caulibus, an Italian Franciscan friar and
preacher.[15] He writes for a Poor Clare nun from Tuscany in
order to introduce her to a way of meditation. She is invited
to imaginatively consider the humanity of Jesus so as to arrive at a contemplation of Christ's divinity. Most important
for our consideration here is the fact that Caulibus gives directives for the nun's spiritual growth according to Franciscan virtues.

In the Prologue to the *Meditations*, Caulibus contends
there is no better school against vice than in the life of the
Lord Jesus, "a life that was absolutely perfect and without
any defect." While habitual meditation brings a familiarity
with and love for Christ's life, such meditation, above all,
strengthens and instructs the soul "with regard to what it
should do and what it should avoid doing."[16] While the dichot-
omy is somewhat anachronistic, we can say that Caulibus's
meditations are both spiritual and moral in nature. Caulibus
elaborates to his Poor Clare reader that the life of Christ

---

[14] Zachary Hayes, *The Hidden Center: Spirituality and Speculative
Christology in St. Bonaventure* (St. Bonaventure, NY: The Franciscan Institute, 2000), 139.

[15] In addition to the introduction to the *Meditations*, see a brief chapter on John of Caulibus by C. Mary Stallings-Taney in *Jesus: The Complete
Guide*, ed. J. Leslie Houlden (London: Continuum, 2006).

[16] John of Caulibus, *Meditations on the Life of Christ*, trans. Francis
X. Taney, Sr., Anne Miller, and C. Mary Stallings-Taney (Asheville, NC:
Pegasus Press, 2000), Prologue, 1.

teaches about what must be done so that neither enemies nor vices can make inroads or deceive you: this by reason of the fact that the perfection of virtues is found right there. Where else will you find examples and teachings of charity, of the most exalted kind of poverty, of exceptional humility, of profound wisdom, of prayer, of kindness, of obedience, of patience, and of all the other virtues, like those found in the life of the Master of all virtues?[17]

Before concluding the Prologue, Caulibus remarks that it was through meditation and the habitual association with the Lord Jesus that Blessed Francis arrived at his abundant virtues and could recognize the vices and deceits of the enemy, thus becoming a mirror of Christ's life. Indeed, Caulibus broadly recommends this contemplation since the Lord is the mirror model for us all.[18] Over the course of the meditations, special consideration is given to the virtues of poverty, humility, and charity as well as the vices of pride, sensuality, and idle curiosity.

Poverty is identified at the very beginning of Christ's life. Caulibus invites meditation on the "wretched poverty" of the mother and child among the animals and hay in a lowly stable.[19] In another chapter devoted to imaginative consideration of the gift of the Magi, Caulibus perceives a "clarion call for poverty." First, Jesus and his mother received the alms as paupers. Second, they were unwilling to keep what they received. Within a few days' time, our Lady gave all the riches away to the poor in her zealousness for poverty. Thus, "the desire for poverty grew steadily" in mother and child.[20] In their flight into Egypt, the family traveled in a foreign land as poor people owning nothing; but they loved poverty and remained faithful to it their entire lives.[21]

Caulibus explains the virtue of poverty as having and wishing for nothing that is beyond necessity. Though he

---

[17] John of Caulibus, *Meditations on the Life of Christ*, Prologue, 2.
[18] John of Caulibus, *Meditations on the Life of Christ*, Ch. 15, 60.
[19] John of Caulibus, *Meditations on the Life of Christ*, Ch. 7, 25.
[20] John of Caulibus, *Meditations on the Life of Christ*, Ch. 9, 35.
[21] John of Caulibus, *Meditations on the Life of Christ*, Ch. 12, 42-48.

writes for a nun who has already taken the vow of poverty, he offers this virtue as something distinct from material want. He explains, "The poverty of which I speak is rooted in the heart, for virtues are to be set in the soul, not in externals. You make your vow of poverty best, then if your agreement is in the heart."[22] He explains that poverty can be troublesome and can even foster interior cupidity if it is merely living in need. In the inevitable "mire of desires" and "weight of greed" it is not possible to rise to the purity of God and heavenly things. Poverty is virtuous when it is loved, that is, when it is voluntary and taken up for the love of God. Caulibus identifies poverty as the Lord's most exalted virtue and as the main foundation of the entire spiritual edifice since poverty unencumbers a person of the burden of temporal affairs and allows the spirit to rise to God.[23]

Humility is closely associated with poverty.[24] Thus, Jesus is not only the "lover of poverty" but the "master of humility."[25] Caulibus suggests a meditation on the little known youth of Jesus to recommend this virtue. Acknowledging that his material comes from neither Scripture nor the holy doctors, Caulibus alleges that the young Jesus appeared in public as "useless, of low estate and stupid."[26] While people expected him to be a man of accomplishment, this imposing young man did nothing worthy of note. He withdrew from company and conversation and remained in prayer in the lower section of church. By accomplishing nothing, Jesus "was presenting himself as despicable to all."[27] He did not wish to be well-regarded and longed to be an outcast of no account. Caulibus deems this humility to be the stabilizing foundation of all the virtues, a fitting sword to bring the haughty low. Beyond the unremarkable youth of Jesus, humility is observed

---

[22] John of Caulibus, *Meditations on the Life of Christ*, Ch. 44, 145.

[23] John of Caulibus, *Meditations on the Life of Christ*, Ch. 7, 25.

[24] John of Caulibus, *Meditations on the Life of Christ*, Chs. 7, 9: 24-29, 33-36.

[25] John of Caulibus, *Meditations on the Life of Christ*, Ch. 24, 94.

[26] John of Caulibus, *Meditations on the Life of Christ*, Ch. 15, 56.

[27] John of Caulibus, *Meditations on the Life of Christ*, Ch. 15, 57.

"in each and every one of his actions"[28]: in setting out on his ministry as a servant, barefoot and alone,[29] in submitting to baptism by John and appearing as a sinner, in stripping "like any other humble man" and "immersed in frigid water,"[30] in calling his disciples brothers and in washing their feet.[31] In death, he is humiliated on the cross and even beyond death he judges that that which is done to the least of his brothers has been done to him.[32] Caulibus praises Christ's "ongoing pouring out of self in humility"[33] and so it is clear how this virtue is the fundamental shape of both incarnation and passion. Indeed, of all the virtues, humility is the one most intimately connected to the work of salvation: "For [Christ] knew that just as pride is the beginning of all sin, likewise humility is the foundation of every salvific good…. Therefore, do not place your trust in virginity or poverty or in any virtue or work, without humility."[34]

Humility is for Caulibus the foundation of all virtue. Among Franciscans, he is certainly not alone; Thomas of Celano and Bonaventure are just two who echo this claim. Yet, even with humility as the foundation, charity remains the form of the virtues. This is first evident in how Caulibus regards humility itself. He appropriates a distinction made by Bernard of Clairvaux between humility produced by truth and humility which charity builds and sets afire. Truth humiliates and reveals how lowly we are. However, the humility built by charity requires that we actively will to appear as we are and we exalt God instead of ourselves.[35] In another chapter, Caulibus depicts Mary's anointing of the feet of Jesus and praises the charity displayed by the Lord in this exchange. With freedom of spirit and gratuitous goodness, Christ extends himself to every neighbor from a bounty

---

[28] John of Caulibus, *Meditations on the Life of Christ*, Ch. 16, 72.
[29] John of Caulibus, *Meditations on the Life of Christ*, Ch. 16, 63.
[30] John of Caulibus, *Meditations on the Life of Christ*, Ch. 16, 71.
[31] John of Caulibus, *Meditations on the Life of Christ*, Ch. 15, 59.
[32] John of Caulibus, *Meditations on the Life of Christ*, Ch. 15, 59.
[33] John of Caulibus, *Meditations on the Life of Christ*, Ch. 15, 58.
[34] John of Caulibus, *Meditations on the Life of Christ*, Ch. 15, 59.
[35] John of Caulibus, *Meditations on the Life of Christ*, Ch. 16, 64-65.

of love and good will. Charity embraces all people, even when there is no obligation or advantage, and it seeks no retribution from the guilty. Thus, "charity reestablishes peace between God and man."[36] Charity informs all virtues because it strives for true union and loving solidarity among creation and between creation and God. In addition to the virtues of poverty, humility, and charity, Caulibus also gives special consideration to patience, obedience, discretion, silence, and prayer. I will return to a number of these later. I turn now to the vices featured in Caulibus's meditations.

Caulibus asserts that humility is the virtue "we need the most" since it makes war upon pride, "the enemy of all grace."[37] Pride is the chief and most insidious vice since it aggrandizes itself with the good work coming from other virtues. Only humility can resist this. While pride is the chief vice, Caulibus also makes reference to sensuality, ambition, vanities, idleness, and loquacity[38] – all of which speak to a concern for tending to things inferior to the holy matters of God. He is influenced in part by the concerns of the Poor Clare nun for whom he writes. For example, Caulibus considers the dangerous vice which is the spending of time on vain, frivolous activities such as sewing objects of art.[39] These idle curiosities are causes of pride and they withdraw the soul from God, wishing to please the creature more than the Creator. With these and other vices, Caulibus demonstrates a deeply Franciscan concern with a humble and single-minded stance of praise toward God. The meditations of Caulibus lead to the conclusion that humility and pride are the preeminent Franciscan virtue and vice, respectively.

---

[36] John of Caulibus, *Meditations on the Life of Christ*, Ch. 28, 100.

[37] John of Caulibus, *Meditations on the Life of Christ*, Ch. 16, 70, 72.

[38] John of Caulibus, *Meditations on the Life of Christ*, Chs. 4, 8, 12, 35: 13-17, 30-32, 42-48, 113-19.

[39] John of Caulibus, *Meditations on the Life of Christ*, Ch. 12, 46-47.

OPPOSITIONAL NATURE OF FRANCISCAN VIRTUE

A corollary of the Christological basis for Franciscan virtue is the dramatic opposition between virtue and vice. The exemplary virtue of Christ is not mere instruction but also a means of salvation. One commentator of Bonaventure's theology of the cross observes that "God in Christ overcomes pride by being humble, disobedience by being obedient, destruction as final word through forgiveness, ... and death through life."[40] In the Franciscan moral landscape, virtue and vice are not merely opposites; they are opposed, caught up in conquest of good over evil. Francis's own *Salutation of the Virtues* is clear evidence of the dynamic of battle between virtue and vice: "Holy Wisdom confounds Satan and all his cunning ... holy Poverty confounds the desires for riches, greed, and the cares of this world. Holy Humility confounds pride ..."[41] Francis describes the function of all the virtues in negative terms: their function is simply to destroy vice.[42] Chapter XXVII of the *Admonitions*, renders a similar function for the various virtues made apparent in its title, "Virtue Puts Vice to Flight."[43]

Repeatedly, talk of virtue and vice employs images of battle, conquest, and defeat. The 1228 papal document declaring Francis a saint speaks of how the Poor Man of Assisi uprooted his vices and took up struggle against the world, renouncing all matter of things that would prevent him from advancing up the steps of virtue toward the house of God. Bonaventure continues this imagery, describing in one of his sermons how "Saint Francis strove with constant sighs of sorrow to root out vice and sin totally from the field of

---

[40] Dreyer, 194.

[41] Francis of Assisi, *A Salutation of the Virtues*, in *FA:ED* 1, 164-65.

[42] Only the last virtue, Holy Obedience, is supplemented with a few lines of more constructive, positive language: "Holy Obedience ... binds its mortified body to obedience of the Spirit and obedience to one's brother, so that it is subject and submissive to everyone in the world, not only to people but to every beast and wild animal as well that they may do whatever they want with it insofar as it has been given to them from above by the Lord." *A Salutation of the Virtues*, in *FA:ED* 1, 164-65.

[43] *FA:ED* 1, 136-37.

his heart."[44] The eradication of vice necessarily precedes the acquisition of any virtue. In his *Collationes in Hexaemeron* (*Collations on the Six Days*), Bonaventure also echoes the negative function of virtue, listing clearly the several carnal and spiritual vices that are removed by the various virtues. Temperance removes gluttony and luxury; munificence removes avarice and cupidity; fortitude removes spiritual disgust and sloth; meekness removes anger; and so forth. [45] We find this dynamic clearly in John of Caulibus as well. He calls for an intense and steady warfare against gluttony[46] as well as "warfare against pride."[47]

Therefore, I suggest that a characteristic feature of Franciscan discourse is found in the reaction of virtue against vice. Expressed another way, vice determines virtue. Because of pride, Christ was humble since it is the disease that determines the remedy. The structure of Franciscan virtue is not based on the positive perfection of human powers; rather, it is based on a notion of human vice. That understanding of vice is then coupled with the virtue of Christ through which vice was ultimately defeated – and by which we are to defeat vice in imitation.

As demonstrated through the work of John of Caulibus, pride is the chief vice. The severe language of Francis regarding the evil of self-will[48] and his praise of the virtue of humility corroborates this claim. Bonaventure echoes this as well. In his *Life of St. Francis*, or *Major Legend*, pride is the

---

[44] Bonaventure of Bagnoregio, *The Morning Sermon on St. Francis, 1255*, in *FA:ED* 2, 511.

[45] Temperance removes gluttony and luxury; munificence removes avarice, cupidity, and rapacity; fortitude removes spiritual disgust, sloth, and laziness; meekness removes anger, hatred, and impatience; kindness removes evil; and magnanimity removes pride, arrogance, vanity, and pretense. *The Collations on the Six Days*, 5.11, 80-81.

[46] John of Caulibus, *Meditations on the Life of Christ*, Ch. 44, 147.

[47] John of Caulibus, *Meditations on the Life of Christ*, Ch. 16, 70.

[48] See Admonitions II "The Evil of Self-Will," *FA:ED* 1, 129, and III "Perfect Obedience" in which he describes how some religious "return to the vomit of their own will," *FA:ED* 1, 130.

"source of all evil"[49] and thus humility is "the guardian and the ornament of all the virtues."[50] In his laud entitled "Pride, the Root of All Sins," late thirteenth century Franciscan Jacopone da Todi colorfully depicts this central vice: "The proud man seeks to subject the world to himself, wants to look up to no one at all, nor can he find strength to take joy in his equals. With unruly heart he oppresses the weak, for they could never pay him sufficient honor."[51] The vice of pride is thus insatiable, spawning all sorts of evil (for Jacopone: anger, cruelty, sloth, avarice, etc.).

It can be little surprise, then, that the Franciscan life of virtue is frequently associated with the notion of cleansing. The structure of Bonaventure's *Major Legend* offers just one example. Situated within a chronological frame of Francis's life are nine thematic chapters based on the virtues. These nine are taken according to three divisions which correspond to the three ascending stages of the spiritual life: purgation, illumination, and perfection.[52] Those virtues most properly understood as virtuous habits tend to occupy the lower two levels of this progression. Austerity, chastity, humility, obedience, and poverty comprise the purgative stage; piety and charity occupy the earlier levels of the stage of illumination. Instead of interpreting all nine levels as depicting virtue, one might instead perceive a progression from virtue, then to gifts, and finally to beatitude. This is a progression offered by Bonaventure himself in the *Breviloquium*.[53] Parallel to this spiritual-moral progression seems to be to another progression: virtues that can be acquired by voluntary choices of the human will lead increasingly to those gifts and perfections that can only be given as graces through the will of God. Per-

---

[49] Bonaventure, *The Life of St. Francis*, Ch. 6.11, in *Bonaventure: The Soul's Journey into God – The Tree of Life – The Life of St. Francis*, ed. Ewert Cousins (Mahwah, NJ: Paulist Press, 1978), 237.

[50] Bonaventure, *The Life of St. Francis*, Ch. 6.1, *FA:ED* 2, 228.

[51] Jacopone da Todi, *The Lauds*, No. 14, trans. Serge and Elizabeth Hughes (New York: Paulist Press, 1982), 92.

[52] Ewert Cousins, "Introduction" in *Bonaventure: The Soul's Journey into God – The Tree of Life – The Life of St. Francis*, 42-45.

[53] *The Breviloquium*, V, Ch. 4-6, 193-206.

haps it is most fitting to consider Franciscan virtue and vice as a subset of Franciscan spirituality, a subset distinguished by a concern for those spiritual goods for which we have the greatest moral responsible. One seems to be culpable for a lack of humility in a way that one is not for a lack of the Stigmata, the highest level in Bonaventure's *Major Legend* progression.

II. FRANCISCAN VIRTUE AND THE CARDINAL VIRTUES

If we simply leave virtue and vice to the realm of contemplation, we can be content with the offerings of John of Caulibus and consider our work nearly complete. However, I have included Bonaventure in this project quite deliberately. While the Seraphic Doctor offers a vision of virtue and vice in his spiritual works, one which resonates in many ways with the later meditations of Caulibus, Bonaventure also considers virtue in his more philosophical writings. I will introduce some of this work briefly so that we might create a bridge between the spiritual and philosophical accounts. Indeed, it is important to note that the Franciscan tradition not only uplifts virtues of humility, poverty, and obedience, but also gives an important place to the traditional four cardinal virtues.

How do we relate Franciscan virtues to the cardinal virtues?

Although I began with a claim that Franciscan virtues are fundamentally Christological rather than anthropological, I must at this point introduce a bit of nuance to that statement. Christ as exemplar shows humans who and what to imitate and thus how to proceed on the path to perfection; therefore, Christology becomes the basis for anthropology. Although its starting point is found in Christ, Franciscan virtue is necessarily anthropological since it shows us true human fulfillment. It is simply that, for Francis and his successors, Christ reveals human fulfillment in a way that we might not otherwise discover through mere contemplation of the nature of humans.

Just as Bonaventure considers the summit of all virtue in Christ, he also adopts an anthropological consideration of the virtues in the course of his philosophical writings. In the *Breviloquium*, the four cardinal virtues set the soul aright. "Prudence rectifies the rational faculties, fortitude the irascible appetite, temperance the concupiscible appetite, while justice directs all of these powers in their relation to a given person."[54]

The *Collations on the Six Days* record Bonaventure's discussion of the cardinal virtues. This text comes from evening talks given near the end of Bonaventure's life when he was no longer teaching at the university. While this text exhibits "an extravagantly symbolic mode of expression" his presentation of the cardinal virtues is consistent with earlier works such as his commentary on the *Sentences* and the *Breviloquium*.[55]

In the Collations, Bonaventure summarizes the four levels in which the cardinal virtues participate as they were identified by the philosophers:[56] the social virtues, the cleansing virtues, the virtues for those already cleansed, and the exemplary virtues. Although they appear to originate in humans, Bonaventure corrects the philosophers by identifying God as the origin of the virtues; the cardinal virtues are "impressed upon the soul" by the divine exemplary light.[57] Thus, the cardinal virtues are properly found in God and humans participate in these virtues by various degrees.[58] Only through illumination by the three theological virtues of faith, hope, and love can the cardinal virtues attain their final perfection. As Kent Emery notes, Bonaventure teaches that the

---

[54] *The Breviloquium*, V, Ch. 4.5, 195.

[55] Kent Emery, Jr., "Reading the World Rightly and Squarely: Bonaventure's Doctrine of the Cardinal Virtues," *Traditio* 39 (1983): 183-218.

[56] Bonaventure takes issue with Aristotle, however, who denied the idea of divine exemplars. See *The Collations on the Six Days*, 6.10, 99; Emery, 206-7.

[57] *The Collations on the Six Days*, 6.10, 99.

[58] "Likewise, in the soul there are lesser virtues whose function is to retain light, lest it run through; there are intermediate virtues that act like polishes; and there are higher virtues like crowning brightness: and in this sense the soul is a mirror." *The Collations on the Six Days*, 5.25, 88.

cardinal virtues are planted in man's social nature and lead from moral purgation to contemplation to the light of highest vision.[59] I suggest that Bonaventure, in his more philosophical writing, sets up the cardinal virtues in a somewhat parallel position to those virtues we observed in the purgative stage of the spiritual ascent of the *Major Legend*. These are all cleansing virtues which then lead upward toward fulfillment and perfection.

Though quite briefly, Caulibus refers to the four cardinal virtues in his meditations, remarking that the Lord of virtues employed these four for our instruction. He goes on to assert that all other moral virtues depend on these four.[60] Bonaventure makes a similar claim, explaining that the cardinal virtues are the entrance to all virtues and, moreover, have all the other moral virtues contained within them.[61] Thus, considering the parallel structure I have just suggested between Bonaventure's cardinal virtues and his purgative virtues of the *Major Legend*, I further suggest that there may be a specific correlation between each cardinal virtue and a virtue characteristic of Franciscan writings. I will attempt to demonstrate below that humility pertains to justice, patience to fortitude, and poverty to temperance. Prudence offers a more complicated correlation which will be treated separately below.

In Bonaventure and John of Caulibus, justice and humility are linked with one another. For instance, in the *Disputed Questions on Evangelical Perfection*, Bonaventure speaks of humility as giving due honor and worship to God as well as giving what is due to other human beings. As a result, Bonaventure renders humility as the summit of all Christian perfection.[62] Caulibus, with a reference to the Gospel of Matthew 3:15, states that the humility shown by Christ as he bowed low before John the Baptist was a fulfillment and

---

[59] Emery, 212.

[60] John of Caulibus, *Meditations on the Life of Christ*, Ch. 70, 221.

[61] John of Caulibus, *The Collations on the Six Days*, 6.11, 100.

[62] Dreyer, 201 discusses Bonaventure's *Disputed Questions on Evangelical Perfection*, 1.

perfection of justice. Caulibus explains to the Poor Clare nun that the humble man "renders to everyone his due: he does not snatch for himself what belongs to another but rather gives honor to God, and keeps for himself his own lowliness. You will better understand this if you consider the injustice of the proud man, who attributes the good gifts of God to himself."[63] Humility, then, is to know who we are in relation to God. It is the virtue that does justice to the relationship between the infinitely good God and the finite and flawed (yet beloved) creature. Indeed, the humility of Christ enacted this justice in a particular way, by reconciling God and God's fallen creation. Caulibus notes that the humble man refrains from judging his neighbor; justice demands this it would seem. While we know our own faults, we cannot truly know the heart of our neighbor. Moreover, in the face of God's great goodness it seems impossible to judge among sinners. Humility pertains to and perfects justice because it truly recognizes oneself as well as God. Considering the humble servant of God, Francis notes that "what a person is before God, that he is and no more."[64] Humility fulfills justice by seeking due praise of God rather than praise of self.[65]

I turn next to fortitude which I identify in the Franciscan virtue of patience. As Caulibus constructs a meditation on the flight into Egypt during Jesus' young life, he encourages his reader to have patience when she is troubled. Jesus gave no dispensation from suffering to either himself or his mother so we must also be willing to suffer persecution with patience and avoid retaliation or taking the offensive.[66] Similarly, it was the Lord's patience that allowed him to be handled by the gory beast as when it placed him at the top of a mountain to tempt him during his fast in the desert.[67] Thomas of Celano speaks of the virtue of patience in a similar

---

[63] John of Caulibus, *Meditations on the Life of Christ*, Ch. 16, 66.

[64] Francis of Assisi, *The Admonitions*, Ch. XIX, in *FA:ED* 1, 135.

[65] One can imagine that if the vice to be destroyed were not pride but rather self-denigration, the phrase would in that case read "what a person is before God, that he is and no less."

[66] John of Caulibus, *Meditations on the Life of Christ*, Ch. 12, 43.

[67] John of Caulibus, *Meditations on the Life of Christ*, Ch. 17, 76.

way, detailing how Francis and his companions in the Order of Lesser Brothers suffered persecution, especially of their bodies. They endured abuses of mockery, insult, stripping, being beaten and jailed, etc. without defending themselves; "they endured all of these abuses so bravely that from their mouths came only the sound of praise and thanksgiving."[68] In the *Collations*, Bonaventure speaks of the virtue of fortitude with identical language. The virtue of fortitude endures with constancy in the face of attack or confrontation[69]; it prevents the soul from withdrawing in fear or terror.[70]

Third, we come to the virtue of poverty as the Franciscan virtue pertaining to temperance. At one point in Bonaventure's *Collations*, he invokes temperance as that which concerns giving up all the things the body demands, to the extent nature allows it.[71] This profound surrendering of material goods clearly resonates with the virtue of voluntary poverty. Elsewhere in the *Collations*, in fact, Bonaventure defends poverty as abiding by the rule of temperance. Caulibus, for his part, especially applies the virtue of poverty to issues of food, abstinence, and the resistance of gluttony,[72] and he remarks how poverty requires the distinction between pleasure and health. Thus, poverty is well-suited as the Franciscan version of temperance, a virtue which is centrally concerned with pleasure and desire.

In light of these associations, I suggest an approach to Franciscan virtue in which one seeks justice through humility, fortitude through patience, and temperance through poverty.

As I mentioned above, prudence requires a more complex treatment. Prudence is that which guides or moderates the other moral virtues, assigning the means to the ends determined by justice, fortitude, and temperance. I identify Fran-

[68] Thomas of Celano, *The Life of Saint Francis*, Bk. 1, Ch. XV, in *FA:ED* 1, 219.
[69] *The Collations on the Six Days*, 6.17, 102.
[70] *The Collations on the Six Days*, 6.26, 105.
[71] *The Collations on the Six Days*, 6.26, 105.
[72] John of Caulibus, *Meditations on the Life of Christ*, Ch. 44, 144-55.

ciscan prudence as an affective collaboration of the virtues of discretion and obedience. Caulibus mentions prudence specifically in his meditations within the context of the bodily hardship and abstinence he associates with poverty. Considering the example of Jesus even in his infancy, Caulibus praises the affliction of the body and, with Luke's Go and do likewise, he encourages his reader to imitate Christ "but prudently" he says, "so that you do not exceed your own powers."[73] In a later meditation on poverty, he explains how virtuous abstinence turns to vice in three situations: when practiced contrary to the will of a superior, when it would cause scandal to one's community, and when "done beyond what the body can bear."[74] He goes on to speak of an illuminating light of discretion "which is the mother of virtues and the consummation of perfection." It appears this virtue of discretion is Caulibus's virtue of prudence as it determines virtue by bearing in mind the limits of one's own capacity. He explains how discretion "undoubtedly teaches us not to overdo anything, and this is as the eighth day on which the boy is circumcised (Luke 2:21), because it is true discretion that circumcises, so that neither too much nor too little is done." Yet prudence not only responds to one's own limits but the limits created by one's relationship to both superiors and the community at large. As a result of this latter component, the Franciscan prudence of Caulibus is not only discretion but also obedience as well. Invoking the work of Bernard of Clairvaux, he explains that "since discretion is such a rare bird on earth, fill its place with the virtue of obedience, brothers, so that you do nothing other than what has been commanded."[75] Obedience becomes a kind of shorthand for personal discretion since it is not only our own limits by which we must abide. Much like humility, there is a deep sense of relationality at work in Franciscan prudence. These virtues are attained in light of the relationship to God and others; there can be no sense of an isolated perfection of human capability. Of course, the starting point

---

[73] John of Caulibus, *Meditations on the Life of Christ*, Ch. 7, 27.

[74] John of Caulibus, *Meditations on the Life of Christ*, Ch. 44, 152.

[75] John of Caulibus, *Meditations on the Life of Christ*, Ch.44, 155.

of Franciscan virtue is itself relational, first drawing us out into the imitation of Christ rather than an initial inward turn to the natural human powers and appetites.

Prudence is not only relational but affective as well. We not only judge in terms of personal capacity and communal need or command, we must also judge through love and delight. Caulibus again explains through the issue of poverty: "Love poverty in your heart ... Have nothing and wish to have nothing beyond necessity. If you inquire what that necessity seeks, I will reply that the more intimately you have loved poverty, the more accurately you will judge necessity."[76] If we judge the means of virtue fittingly, we will take delight in it. Caulibus does not negate the role of reason in judgment, but adds to it the necessary qualification of joy and delight. If we are indiscreet in our practice of virtue, we become distracted by desires and can take no delight in the poverty, patience, or humility that we show. At one point, Caulibus quotes Bernard who calls for both discretion as well as the fervor of charity.[77] And thus, without regard to the necessarily affective quality of prudence, without love or joy in what such prudence prescribes, any virtue turns to vice.

Bonaventure also includes Aristotle in his discussion of prudence. He acknowledges the Aristotelian mean which finds an intermediate point between two extremes, as the wise man will prescribe.[78] Quoting Augustine's term for the mean as "proper measure," Bonaventure arrives at prudence as the virtue which drives all other virtues and finds proper measure "so that you do not go too far in anything, but remain close to the center."[79] While Bonaventure's more philosophical prudence shares much with the discretion we have found in Caulibus, it lacks the relational and affective quali-

---

[76] John of Caulibus, *Meditations on the Life of Christ*, Ch. 44, 145.

[77] John of Caulibus, *Meditations on the Life of Christ*, Ch. 44, 154.

[78] A common example of the mean between the extremes is the mean of courage or fortitude between cowardice and foolhardiness or recklessness.

[79] Bonaventure of Bagnoregio, *Collations on the Six Days*, 6.12, The Works of Bonaventure V, José de Vinck, tr. (Paterson, NJ: St. Anthony Guild Press, 1970), 100.

ties which I suggest make for a particularly Franciscan version of the virtue. This leads us to the question of whether Franciscan virtue is, on the whole, truly compatible with the Aristotelian mean.

Does Franciscan virtue abide by the Aristotelian mean?

Francis has been identified by many as a saint of excesses. As the founder of Franciscan spirituality, this can helpfully point to the radical Gospel life of Francis, Clare, and those who have been inspired by them. However, in terms of virtue and vice, the notion of excess seems troubling indeed. Aristotle had long before defined virtue as the mean between extremes, a definition taken to heart by Thomas Aquinas and others. What place is there for this mean between extremes in Franciscan virtue?

Bonaventure speaks of the temptations of pleasure and passion and how they are the death of humans who desire to possess them. It is wrong he asserts to consider such things to be the greatest good and yet is also wrong to consider them as the greatest evil.[80] The mean or middle way "is not a matter of things, but of the soul's desire. For if you desire these things in order to be sustained by them, be they your own or those of others, you keep the middle way."[81] Thus, Bonaventure contends that poverty does in fact keep to the mean. Indeed he goes on to draw quite the analogy! To accuse the excessively poor as violating the mean is the same as suggesting that sexual abstinence lacks virtue. It is the same as suggesting that the mean is found in having relations with half of all the women in the world which would be the middle way between all the women and no women at all.[82]

Bonaventure is helpful in making this distinction between the mean of material things and the mean of desire. The criterion of sustenance – what the person needs and

---

[80] *Collations on the Six Days*, 5.3, 75.
[81] *Collations on the Six Days*, 5.4, 76.
[82] *Collations on the Six Days*, 5.5, 78.

what the person can handle – is reminiscent of the discretion we found in Caulibus. The missing relationality and affectivity are supplied by a different sort of mean, one which appears at the very start of Bonaventure's *Collations*. Christ is the center, the mediator, the middle way.[83] The second person of the Trinity is the mean between each of God's three operations [emanation, exemplarity, and consummation] and the created world.[84] Christ constitutes the center or mean in various orders, one among which is the order of moderation. Bonaventure remarks this is an order of great importance given its role in the choice of moral good. Referencing Aristotle's *Ethics*, he concludes that the faith that is at the center and foundation of all virtue can be compared to the center identified by Aristotle "as that which determines right reason."[85] And so it appears that the Aristotelian mean is in fact compatible with Franciscan virtue. Yet, while not contradicting right reason, reason itself is not the primary standard for such virtue. The mean is in Christ who is the middle way between God and the world. Thus, we have relationship and affectivity. We find the mean in relationship to Christ who in turn is the key to the relationship between God and creation. And we find the mean when Christ's example orders us to our proper end: an affective delight in and love of God.

III. THE END OF FRANCISCAN VIRTUE

Before attempting to bring together a final vision of this Franciscan virtue approach, it is necessary to identify the end to which such virtues are ultimately oriented. Along with Aquinas and countless others, Franciscan virtue perceives that charity, union with God, is our end and the form of the virtues. Yet, what seems characteristically Franciscan is the role of joy and delight which accompanies this charity. Whereas Aquinas can speak of a twofold happiness – an imperfect happiness in this life and the perfect happiness that

---

[83] John of Caulibus, *Meditations on the Life of Christ*, 1.1, 1.

[84] Emery, 199; see *The Collations on the Six Days*, 3.2, 42.

[85] *The Collations on the Six Days*, 1.33, 17.

is our ultimate life in God, Franciscan virtue directs itself
not to happiness but instead to joy. Franciscan virtue speaks
of delight even and especially in the midst of suffering. This
is the true and perfect joy of St. Francis who, cold, tired, in-
sulted, and rejected, was still able to bear with patience and
give thanks to God. This, Francis tells Brother Leo, is true joy
as well as true virtue.[86] Thomas of Celano describes the narrow lodging where Francis and his companions stayed. There
was no grumbling but with a peaceful heart "the soul filled
with joy preserved the virtue of patience."[87]

Similarly, John of Caulibus offers the examples of Francis
and Clare who "emerged from their many tribulations, wants
and infirmities not only long-suffering but even cheerful."[88]
In numerous meditations he emphasizes how Jesus, his
mother, and the disciples, suffered but suffered joyfully.[89] For
Bonaventure, the difference between the philosophers' cardinal virtues and those illuminated by faith, involves affective
disposition. Only the Physician Christ heals the affective dispositions through charity.[90] It is divine love that makes fear
holy, sorrow just, joy true, and trust assured.[91]

Joy and delight are crucial for the fulfillment of all virtues. Indeed, the language of delight often seems to animate
the Franciscan virtue more than the language of union.[92] Joy
is the ability to praise God in all times and conditions. Thus,
for Franciscan virtue, human flourishing seems not an end
in itself but a means toward achieving the capacity to praise
and delight in God. In Thomas of Celano's *First Life*, Francis

---

[86] Francis of Assisi, *True and Perfect Joy*, in *FA:ED* 1, 166-67.

[87] Thomas of Celano, *The Life of Saint Francis*, Bk. 1, Ch. XVI, in
FA:ED 1, 220.

[88] John of Caulibus, *Meditations on the Life of Christ*, Prologue, 2.

[89] See, for example, *Meditations on the Life of Christ*, Ch. 7, Ch. 44: 26,
144.

[90] *The Collations on the Six Days*, 7.14, 116.

[91] *The Collations on the Six Days*, 7.7, 112-14.

[92] For example, see Quinn, "The Moral Philosophy of St. Bonaventure,"
29.

and his companions "never or hardly ever stopped praying and praising God."[93]

IV. CONCLUDING REFLECTIONS

Having begun this investigation with Christ's suffering as the source of virtue and having arrived at delight in God as virtue's aim, I conclude now with four points of reflection that can help us to identify the continuing contribution and significance of Franciscan virtue and vice.

First, the starting point of Franciscan virtue is in Christ, not in an anthropological structure of human powers or abilities. This explains the many legitimate permutations in which these virtues appear. It also gives us leave to continue to innovate new ways to think about and apply the rich models of Francis and Clare, which themselves are finite attempts at living out the infinitely profound model of God among us. I have suggested one possible approach here which strives to integrate the traditional cardinal virtues and the Aristotelian mean with the spiritually purgative and seemingly excessive virtues found in the lives of Christ and Francis.

Second, the function of Franciscan virtue is to destroy and drive out the prior Franciscan vices. While it is certainly true that these virtues comprise a positive role in the life of moral progress and spiritual ascent, the identity and content of these virtues are determined by and presume particular vices. This is crucial. Otherwise talk of humility, patience, poverty, and obedience, should make us very nervous indeed. With these virtues guiding us, do we not lose the prophetic call for justice for the poor? With these virtues, would women be voting? Is this not what Martin Luther King, Jr. railed against in his Letter from the Birmingham jail?[94] This call

---

[93] Thomas of Celano, *The Life of Saint Francis*, Bk. 1, Ch. XV, in *Francis of Assisi: Early Documents*, Vol. 1, 219.

[94] Martin Luther King, Jr., "Letter from the Birmingham Jail," written in response to a letter counseling patience from a group of clergymen

to "wait," be patient, endure hardship? Franciscan virtue is determined by Franciscan vices. We can expect these virtues to seem out of place and even dangerous if we attempt to apply them to a different system of vices. Thus, I suggest that Franciscan virtues are not the virtues of the victims or the oppressed or the powerless, for the vice of the victim is not pride. Franciscan virtues are for those who have power – especially for those who think that their power is deserved and therefore harmless.

Third, I have suggested a set of virtues as a particularly Franciscan version of the traditional cardinal virtues. Franciscan justice is found in humility, Franciscan fortitude in patience, Franciscan temperance in poverty, and Franciscan prudence in a relational and affective discretion. Since these virtues are determined by the vices to which they respond, we can understand that voluntary poverty is directed at those who need to be brought into solidarity with the involuntarily poor. The virtue of poverty is for us as our desires for material goods and seemingly innocent pleasures distract us. They distract us not only from responding to God but to the needs of God's people and all God's creation. The virtue of poverty questions whether our resources are in the control of merely personal desire or at the service of the larger complex of relationships in which we find ourselves. Poverty is not in simple foods because they are the mean of sustenance between undernourishment and luxurious consumption. The virtue of poverty is in asking how and what we should eat in the midst of a world food crisis.

The virtue of patience accepts the reality of struggle and suffering in our world. Patience is for those who would be distracted by one's own might and power, who feel entitled to a life free of hardship. Patience is needed by those who try desperately to deny the fact of illness, aging, and death. Not only our own defects, but the defects of others must be acknowledged. Patience rids us of an indignant self-righteousness which allows us to write one another off at the first sign

on April 16, 1963; available at http://www.africa.upenn.edu/Articles_Gen/Letter_Birmingham.html

of offense. Patience keeps us in relationship. From these de-scriptions of poverty and patience, it is clear how humility shines through and why humility seems the foundation of Franciscan virtue.

The virtue of humility is, I suggest, at the heart of Fran-ciscan justice. It is for those who believe they are self-suffi-cient. The delusion here is twofold: we neither possess self-reliance nor can we ever earn it. As a remedy to this myth of independence and ultimate power, humility is radically relational. Humility is about knowing our place in relation-ship to God, and this in turn tells us our relationship to God's people and the rest of God's creation. Franciscan humility is not simply found in the balance between egoism and self-deprecation; it is a virtue to drive out vice. As such, humility habituates us to look for the injustice that we must overcome because of pride, ambition, etc. Let us note that Bonaventure considers justice as "a disposition which attributes to each one his deserts, once the common good has been served."[95] In justice, humility requires us to see our dependence and that of others. In the first place, we must perceive and strive for the common good.

Franciscan prudence coheres with these virtues since, as already discussed, it requires a truly relational discretion that can at times even require obedience. In addition, it re-quires affectivity, joy, and delight. And so we arrive at the fourth and final point of reflection.

Fourth, the ultimate criterion of Franciscan virtue is not individual human flourishing or happiness, but the ability for praise of and delight in God. Indeed, key Franciscan vices of pride, idleness, and sensuality all concern distractions from giving due praise to God and from finding our joy therein. In-dividual human flourishing is not the standard which makes sense of poverty, patience, or humility. Rather, the standard is delight in God, which is made possible through these vir-tues. We begin to participate in this act of delight and praise through our relationship with God's creation. Thus, it is the

---

[95] *The Collations on the Six Days*, 6.18, 102, my emphasis.

joy found in solidarity that invites all men and women into Franciscan virtue. This is certainly fitting, for it is by that same, very humble solidarity that Christ transformed suffering into true and perfect joy for all.

IS DEATH A MORAL PROBLEM FOR THE FRANCISCAN INTELLECTUAL TRADITION?

Thomas A. Nairn, O.F.M.

Introduction

It was Professor Ilia Delio who suggested that I write on the question whether death is a moral problem for the Franciscan intellectual tradition as it confronts issues raised in medical ethics. I do not think I would have come up with this topic, but I must also admit that ever since I was given the question, I have been intrigued by it. It has taken me to places I normally do not explore, places well outside of my comfort zone within moral theology and medical ethics, and in this paper I would like to share that thought-journey.

There is a short answer and a long answer to the question posed in the title of this paper. The short answer is that for the intellectual tradition of a religious order founded by a person who referred to death as a "sister" and who embraced it lovingly, death simply cannot be a moral problem. However, as we look to the title of this Eleventh Annual Franciscan Symposium "Moral Action in a Complex World: Franciscan Perspectives," a more complicated – shall we say complex – picture emerges: the long answer. Does our Franciscan intellectual tradition have anything to say to the complexity of medical-ethical decision-making regarding end of life issues today? The "long answer" that I would like to explore revolves around the following: At the time when the Franciscan intellectual tradition was developing, little or nothing could be done to prolong life, and thus the medical prolongation of life was not a real issue for the tradition to confront. Nevertheless, those who helped to develop the tradition had a lot to say regarding the nature of death, how one cares for the dying, and whether prolongation of life could be part of this care. The question that faces us today is whether this tradition can enter into conversation with medical ethics as understood in the twenty-first century with its dependence upon technology to prolong life and its involvement in the ethical questions regarding which forms of prolongation are appropriate and which are not. Can the Franciscan intellectual tradition help contemporary medical ethics not only in the question of the ethics of prolonging life but also in that of appropriate care for the dying in a Christian manner?

Embedded in the above statements are four propositions that need to be investigated: (1) that prolongation of life was not an issue at the time of those who began the Franciscan intellectual tradition; (2) that the Franciscan tradition did have something to say about how one ought to care for the dying; (3) that our contemporary experience has been very different from that of the Middle Ages; and (4) that in spite of this difference, contemporary medical ethics can learn something from the Franciscan intellectual tradition. I will try to address each of these propositions in this essay.

MEDICINE IN THE MIDDLE AGES

The prolongation of life as we understand it today was simply not an issue in the Middle Ages. In his classic text on the development of the ordinary/extraordinary distinction in Catholic medical ethics, Daniel Cronin begins his actual discussion of the distinction with the sixteenth century, covering the pre-history of the tradition in the thirteenth through sixteenth centuries in less than a page.[1] Similarly, Darrel Amundsen shows that the understanding that the physician has a duty to prolong life does not arise until the writings of Francis Bacon in the sixteenth century:

Francis Bacon ... in his *De augmentis scientiarum*, divides medicine into three offices: the preservation of health, the cure of diseases, and the prolongation of life. He then writes that "the third part of medicine which I have set down is that which relates to the prolongation of life, which is new, and deficient; and the most noble of all." He protests that physicians have not recognized the significance of the "new" branch of medicine but have confused it with the other two. He urges physicians to investigate means of developing a regimen designed to contribute to longevity.[2]

When one investigates medicine in the Middle Ages, one discovers that it has much more in common with classical conceptions of medicine than with those of the early modern period of European history. The often-quoted line of the Hippocratic corpus could just as appropriately describe the Medieval understanding: "I will define what I conceive medicine to be. In general terms, it is to do away with the sufferings of the sick, to lessen the violence of their diseases, and to refuse to treat those who are overmastered by their diseases, realizing that in such cases medicine is powerless."[3]

Not only did physicians not attempt to prolong life in the Middle Ages, it was considered unethical to do so. The words

---

[1] Daniel A. Cronin, "The Moral Law in Regard to the Ordinary and Extraordinary Means of Conserving Life," in Russell E. Smith, ed., *Conserving Human Life* (Braintree, MA: The Pope John XXIII Center, 1989), 33–34.

[2] Darrel W. Amundsen, *Medicine, Society and Faith in the Ancient and Medieval Worlds* (Baltimore, MD: The Johns Hopkins University Press, 1996), 41-42.

[3] "Selections from the Hippocratic Corpus," in Stanley Joel Reiser, Arthur J. Dyck, and William J. Curran eds., *Ethics in Medicine: Historical Perspectives and Contemporary Concerns* (Cambridge, MA: The MIT Press, 1977), 6.

of Yves Ferroul are instructive here: "A doctor's function is to preserve or restore health, to attend to the living and not to the dead, primarily. People of the Middle Ages were convinced that the physician was called exclusively before death, and the priest at and after demise."[4] In fact, to prolong life was probably considered against the faith. Bernardine of Siena, whom we will soon investigate in greater detail, preached against what he called the "foolish belief that [the dying person] can still evade death."[5]

Furthermore, during the same period of time as the early development of the Franciscan intellectual tradition, physicians themselves acknowledged that one of the tasks of medicine was to ensure that the dying person properly prepared for death. Nancy Saraisi has shown that "unfavorable prognosis would be a signal to turn to religious means of physical healing, to set one's affairs in order, or simply to seek religious consolation."[6] Likewise, Ferroul explains that the statutes of the University of Montpellier, ratified in 1240, "call upon Bachelors of Medicine to swear that they will refuse, in case of grave ailment, to treat the patient who has not first called a priest to his bedside."[7] Physicians cared for the living, and it was not their concern to prolong life. It was the mission of priests and religious to care for the dying and to prepare them for death.

---

[4] Yves Ferroul, "The Doctor and Death in the Middle Ages and the Renaissance," in Edelgard E. DeBruck and Barbara I. Gusick, eds., *Death and Dying in the Middle Ages* (New York: Peter Lang, 1999), 31.

[5] Franco Mormando, "What Happens to Us When We Die? Bernardino of Siena on 'The Four Last Things,'" in DeBruck and Gusick, *Death and Dying in the Middle Ages*, 112. Mormando is quoting from Bernardine's sermon for the Friday after the First Sunday in Lent, *De duodecem doloribus quos patitur peccator in hora mortis.*

[6] Nancy G. Siraisi, *Medieval and Early Renaissance Medicine* (Chicago, IL: University of Chicago Press, 1990), 134.

[7] Ferroul, 40. Ferroul is quoting from Marie-Christine Pouchelle, "La Prise en charge de la mort: medecine, médecins et chirurgiens devant les problèmes liés à la mort à la fin du Moyen Âge (XIIIe-XIVe siècles)," *Archives européennes de sociologie* 17 (1976): 77.

THE FRANCISCAN INTELLECTUAL TRADITION

If this was the state of medicine at the time of the beginnings of the development of the Franciscan intellectual tradition, how does one go about trying to find out how this tradition addressed the issue of death, dying, and the possible prolongation of life? This question led me in a variety of directions. As a moralist, I first looked to some of the tradition's moral writings, especially those of St. Bonaventure, but I soon discovered that the best way to explore the question was to investigate instead the early writings on the Sacrament of the Sick, known then as Extreme Unction, and to the writings on eschatology, that is on the "Last Things." This section on the Franciscan intellectual tradition will therefore consist primarily of an investigation of some of these writings in which I will explore Bonaventure's understanding of death as transitus, his understanding of the resurrection of the body, and his theology of the Sacrament of Extreme Unction. This will be followed by a shorter investigation of one of the sermons of St. Bernardine of Siena, that for the Friday after the First Sunday in Lent, *De duodecem doloribus quos patitur peccator in hora mortis*. I will use these materials to explore the second hypothesis, that the Franciscan tradition did have something to say regarding how one ought to prepare for death.

St. Bonaventure

Daniel Cronin explains that many of the sixteenth and seventeenth century developers of the tradition of ordinary and extraordinary means based their reflection on Thomas Aquinas's discussions of mutilation (ST II-II, q 65, art 1) and especially of suicide (ST II-II, q 64, art 5).[8] It may therefore seem helpful to look at a similar discussion in Bonaventure's *Collations on the Ten Commandments*.[9] In Collation VI, Bo-

---

[8] Cronin, 34.

[9] St. Bonaventure, *Collations on the Ten Commandments*, WSB VI, Introduction and Translation by Paul J. Spaeth (St. Bonaventure NY: The Franciscan Institute, 1995).

naventure states that the last six of the Ten Commandments deal with "blamelessness." Paul Spaeth comments that Bonaventure is using a play on words between "blamelessness" (*innocentiam*) and "harm" (*noceat*).[10] This equation of blamelessness with not doing anything to harm might bring us back to the Hippocratic corpus and possibly to the notion of the morality of prolonging the life of the dying. Among the various distinctions that Bonaventure makes in this collation, he discusses three senses of killing, "either by accident, by necessity, or willfully."[11] When he speaks of willful killing, Bonaventure adds that murder can be committed "in a transferred sense," for example, by not doing something that ought to be done. At first glance this seems to be a possible point of intersection with contemporary medical ethics, especially since Bonaventure quotes St. Ambrose: "Feed the one dying from hunger; if you do not feed him, you have killed him."[12] A more careful reading of the text, however, shows that the omission to which Bonaventure refers is that of starving a healthy person and has nothing to do with end of life issues as understood today.

To a Franciscan moralist then who still feels that he is an outsider when investigating the Franciscan intellectual tradition, it seems that writing about death and dying is not really a concern for Bonaventure, either from an ethical point of view or seemingly from a theological/philosophical one. Hints of his attitude do come across in his writings, however, especially in his writings about what were called the Novissima, the "Last Things," and in his writings about the Sacrament of Extreme Unction. But even here, it seems that one must extrapolate Bonaventure's understanding of death and dying from what he says about other matters, such as his understanding of transitus or that of the resurrection of the

---

[10] *Collations on the Ten Commandments*, 84. The Latin sentence is: *Sequitur de sex aliis mandatis, quae pertinent ad innocentiam, quibus praecipitur, ne quis noceat proximo suo.* See *Opera omnia* Vol. 5, 526a.

[11] *Collations on the Ten Commandments*, 87.

[12] *Collations on the Ten Commandments*, 88. The citation given by Spaeth for this quote is Gratian, *Decretals*, pt. 1 cam. 21, dist. 86.

body. Therefore one moves from moral theology in particular to a larger theological issue, realizing that for St. Bonaventure, as for all theologians in the Middle Ages, theology did not have the strict divisions that we accept today.

Death as *Transitus*

All members of the Franciscan family are familiar with the term transitus, at least as it refers to the ceremony that takes place during the evening of October 3 that commemorates the passing of St. Francis from this world to the next. Therefore they should not be surprised that St. Bonaventure often speaks of death as a transitus, a passing. In an article analyzing the spiritual dimensions of this term, André Ménard speaks of six contexts for the use of the term transitus in the writings of Bonaventure: Besides "death," one sees the theologian using the term in the context of contemplation, the paschal mystery, renunciation, the passing nature of creation and creatures, and the opposition between the transitory and the unchanging.[13]

Ménard argues that the theme of transitus is central to Bonaventure's spiritual theology. He suggests that it forces one to confront the very core of the spiritual life:

> It constantly brings us back to the source of all life: the passion and resurrection of the Lord Jesus. It invites us to become more aware that everything takes place in order that we might enter into the dynamism of the movement initiated by Christ. The meaning of every human adventure is participation with Christ and, in Christ, in the life offered us by God.

---

[13] André Ménard, O.F.M. Cap., "The Spirituality of Transitus in the Writings of St. Bonaventure," *Greyfriars Review* 18, 1 (2004): 24-25. Of fifty-two references to transitus that Ménard cites, he shows that nineteen refer to contemplation, twelve to paschal mystery, twelve to death, six to renunciation, four to the passing nature of creation, and three to the opposition between the transitory and the unchanging.

Part of the understanding of transitus that is important for this study is the passing from what is transitory to what is unchanging.

It is within the context of this that Ménard analyzes Bonaventure's Sermon XIX for the First Sunday of Advent,[14] preached on the words: "Heaven and earth shall pass away, but my words will not pass away" (Luke 21:33). Ménard shows that in this sermon Bonaventure speaks of three forms of passing, each of which is further divided into three parts: the exterior transitus of nature that gives rise to contempt for this world, capacity for rational judgment and a desire for the other world; the interior transitus of grace that moves from evil to good, as from Egypt to the desert, from good to better, as the movement through the desert, and from the better to the best, as passing through the waters of Jordan; and finally the superior transitus to glory.[15] In commenting on the transitus to glory, Ménard explains:

> It is simply the transitus we make through the *reductio integra* that is our death. We return to the Father, the fontal principle of all that is; we enter the sanctuary of wisdom where we discover "the reason of living things" and "the dwellings of the predestined." We enter into loving ecstasy, finding our delight in the contemplation of the one who gives himself to us in his humanity and his divinity. Our happiness is complete.[16]

Thus for Bonaventure transitus demands the leaving of what is passing and the entry into that glory which is the Kingdom of God.

Within this context of transitus from what is passing to what is unchanging, Bonaventure speaks of that transitus that is death. Indeed, in many of the situations in which Bo-

---

[14] See St. Bonaventure, *Opera Omnia*, Volume 9 (Quaracchi: Collegio S. Bonaventurae, 1901), 41-42.

[15] Ménard, 42-43.

[16] Ménard, 44.

naventure uses the term transitus he simply sees it as another word for death itself.[17] It still connotes, however, this movement of passing from what changes and fades into what is eternal. The third chapter of his *Soliloquium*, for example, talks of death within this context. In speaking about the inevitability of death, Bonaventure asks why, when compared to the life to come, do people cling to the life on earth.[18] He then offers the following:

> Oh present life, how you have deceived many! While you pass quickly you are really nothing; while you would see, you are shadow; while you would exalt, you are smoke; you are sweet to the proud, but bitter to those who are wise. Those who love you do not know you; those who understand you flee from you. For some you prolong life, that you might deceive them; to others you make life brief so that you might lead them to despair.[19]

Ménard concludes that life on earth is shadow and deception. True life awaits us in heaven, and it is death which serves as the entry point to glory. St. Bonaventure further notes that while we are on earth we are merely pilgrims:

> According to the etymologies of Jerome and Isidore of Seville, "Hebrew" means "one who is passing through" or "pilgrim." The brothers are the true Hebrews, the true descendents of Abraham in faith.... They too must cross a desert, the world, before arriving in the

---

[17] See, for example, the *Major Legend*: Prol, n. 4; Ch 13, n. 2; Ch 14, n. 2, in *Francis of Assisi: Early Documents*, Vol. 2 *The Founder*, eds. Regis J. Armstrong, J.A. Wayne Hellmann, William J. Short (New York: New City Press, 2000), 528, 631, 641.

[18] See St. Bonaventure, *Opera Omnia*, Vol. 8 (Quaracchi: Collegio S. Bonaventurae, 1898), 52-53.

[19] Ibid. (my translation). The Quaracchi editors indicate that the author of this quote is the author of the sermons to the brothers in the desert.

promised last, heaven. With Jesus they must pass from this world to the Father.[20]

Therefore, taken simply from the point of view of Bonaventure's understanding of transitus, death is far from a problem for the Franciscan intellectual tradition, since it is that which allows the person to pass over from this transitory life to eternal life with God.

The Resurrection of the Body

Reflection upon Bonaventure's use of the notion of transitus shows the positive aspect of his understanding of death. However, looking further into his eschatology, especially investigating his understanding of death as separation of soul and body adds another dimension to the question of the moral status of death in the Franciscan intellectual tradition, one that is more ambiguous. In discussing in his *Breviloquium* the resurrection of the body after the final judgment, Bonaventure suggests that final beatitude "must be brought about in a way that respects the rectitude of justice, the restoration of grace, and the completion of nature." He then suggests that the body must rise in the first place so that, according to justice, "a person be punished or rewarded in both soul and body, for that person has merited or demerited, not in the soul alone, nor in the body alone, but in soul and body together." He goes on to suggest also that "the restoration of grace demands that the entire body be likened to Christ, whose dead body had to rise again because it was inseparable united to his Godhead." Most important from the point of view of this paper, however, is the third element of this triad. Bonaventure states that "the completion of nature demands that human beings be constituted of body and soul, as matter and form mutually need and seek each other."[21]

---

[20] Ménard, 50.

[21] St. Bonaventure, *Breviloquium* Part 7, Chap 5, par 2, WSB IX, Introduction, Translation and Notes by Dominic V. Monti (Saint Bonaventure NY: Franciscan Institute Publications, 2005), 283. Emphasis added.

This understanding of soul and body mutually seeking each other is an important one for Bonaventure. Caroline Walker Bynum, in her classic study on the resurrection of the body, maintains that Bonaventure's understanding of bodily resurrection is based in turn on his understanding of desire.[22] She explains that for Bonaventure this analogy "is not biological but psychological: the love of a man for a woman."[23] Following Michael Schmaus, she further suggests that Bonaventure's argument should be understood as follows: "A complete substance composed of its own form and matter, soul nonetheless needs body for completion; longing for body (appetites, desiderium, inclinatio ad corpus) is thus lodged in its very being."[24] Citing his First Sermon on the Assumption, she further demonstrates that for Bonaventure, "the person is not the soul; it is a composite. Thus it is established that [Mary] must be there [i.e., in heaven] as a composite, that is, of soul and body; otherwise she would not be in perfect joy."[25] The sermon continues: "body must return to soul in order for soul to be perfectly blessed."[26] For Bonaventure, after death – even in heaven – the person will not be completely happy until the resurrection of the body. The *Breviloquium* explains this point further: "Hence, the soul cannot be fully happy unless a body is restored to it, because it has an inclination built into it by nature to be reunited with a body."[27]

From this understanding of blessedness and the resurrection of the body, one begins to understand that for Bonaven-

---

[22] Caroline Walker Bynum, *The Resurrection of the Body in Western Christianity, 200-1336* (New York: Columbia University, 1995), 248.

[23] Bynum, *The Resurrection of the Body*, 237.

[24] Bynum, *The Resurrection of the Body*, 248. Bynum bases her understanding on Michael Schmaus's "Die Unsterblichkeit der Seele und die Auferstehung des Leibes nach Bonaventure," *L'Homme et son destin d'après les penseurs du moyen âge*, Actes du premier Congrès International de Philosophie Médiévale, 1958 (Louvain: Nauwelaerts, 1960), 505-19.

[25] Bynum, *The Resurrection of the Body*, 249, n. 77.

[26] Bynum, *The Resurrection of the Body*, 250.

[27] *Breviloquium*, Part 7, Ch. 7, par 4. (Monti, 294).

ture the soul and the body are involved in mutual desire,[28] a desire that is incomplete until bodily resurrection after the Last Judgment. One may then extrapolate from this understanding of resurrection to ask what death as separation of soul and body must mean for the theologian. John Saward describes how death functions as an important symbol for Bonaventure:

> Bodily death in all its hideousness is not only punishment for sin, it is also, in a certain sense, the terrible symbol of the deformity that is sin. Death is the final ugliness. The body's beauty is destroyed. It decomposes, rots, falls apart. In fact, when no longer informed by the spiritual soul, it is not really a body at all, but a loose amalgam of dissipating elements.... But it is not only the repulsiveness of decomposing flesh that makes death ugly. The separation of immortal soul from mortal body is a marring of the beauty of the whole human nature, which God made to be a unity of matter and spirit. It is a cruel and crude severance. Like St. Thomas, Bonaventure held that the soul separated from the body is not a complete human being.[29]

Thus, for Bonaventure death is ambiguous. It may very well be a theological if not a moral problem. It is an evil in which the soul is most cruelly separated from the body.[30] In a similar context, Bynum refers to "an astonishing passage of the Breviloquium devoted to the crucifixion" in which Bonaventure states that the more perfect a body is, the more

---

[28] Bynum raises questions regarding this mutuality: She shows that "Bonaventure seems sometimes to assert and sometimes to deny that matter yearns also" (Bynum, *The Resurrection of the Body*, 249).

[29] John Saward, "The Flesh Flowers Again: St. Bonaventure and the Aesthetics of the Resurrection," *Downside Review* 110 (January 1992): 4-5.

[30] See Bonaventure's sermon on the 15th Sunday after Pentecost. *Opera omnia*, Vol. IX, 411b. For an English translation see *St. Bonaventure, Sunday Sermons*, WSB XII, edited by Timothy J. Johnson (Saint Bonaventure, NY: Franciscan Institute Publications, 2007), 449-67.

fully it experiences.[31] In Christ's passion, therefore, "because his body possessed perfect physical balance and his senses were in their full vigor, and as his soul possessed perfect love for God and supreme concern for neighbor, his anguish in both body and soul was immeasurable."[32] Death itself becomes part of this anguish. Bonaventure suggests that "since it is precisely the union of body and soul that makes a living human being, it follows that, during those three days [after his death], Christ was not a man, although both his soul and body were united to the Word. But because death in Christ's human nature could not bring death to the person who never ceases to live, death itself perished in life."[33]

Care for the Dying: The Sacrament of Extreme Unction

If death involves such ambiguity, how does one prepare for it? It is interesting that Bonaventure seems to say little about the subject. It is not entirely missing, however. He ends his small treatise *De perfectione vitae ad sorores*, for example, with a discussion on perseverance till death. The last lines of this treatise echo the last part of the *Breviloquium*:

Love God much in this life, and you shall enjoy Him much in the next; let the love of God increase in you now, so that you may have then the fullness of His joy. This is the truth to be pondered in your mind, proclaimed by your tongue, loved in your heart, expressed by your lips; your soul should hunger, your body thirst, your whole substance crave for nothing but this until you enter the joy of your God, until you are clasped in your Lover's arms, until you are led into the chamber of your beloved Spouse, who, with

---

[31] See Bynum, 251.

[32] *Breviloquium*, Part 4, Chap. 9, par 6 (Monti, 163).

[33] *Breviloquium*, Part 4, Chap. 9, par 8 (Monti, 164).

the Father and the Holy Spirit, lives and reigns, one God, forever and ever. Amen.[34]

Ultimately, one prepares for the life to come by living one's earthly life out of longing for God.

The only places where Bonaventure seems to speak directly of care for the dying, however, are in his discussions on the Sacrament of Extreme Unction in the *Sentence Commentary* and in the *Breviloquium*. In the latter work, he defines Extreme Unction as "the sacrament of those departing this life, which prepares and disposes them for the perfect health [of heaven]."[35] Describing the sacrament Bonaventure states that in order for the soul to be made well, "the sacrament must act, and be constituted, received and conferred in a manner that conforms to its end [which is spiritual healing]."[36] He continues:

> First of all, the action of this sacrament should be determined by its end, which is to make the attainment of salvation, that is eternal happiness, swifter and easier for those who receive it. Now this is accomplished by devotion, which raises us up, and by the remission of venial sins and their consequences, which drag us down.[37]

In looking to the constitution of the sacrament, Bonaventure says that since its end is to restore spiritual health through the deliverance from sin, "such health depends in turn on the soundness and purity of the inner conscience upon which the heavenly Judge will pass judgment."[38] Within this context, he stresses the anointing of the parts of the

---

[34] Bonaventure, "On the Perfection of Life Addressed to Sisters," Ch. 8, par 8, in Bonaventure's *Writings on the Spiritual Life*, WSB X, Introduction and Notes by F. Edward Coughlin (Saint Bonaventure, NY: Franciscan Institute Publications, 2007), 194-95.

[35] *Breviloquium*, Part 4, Ch. 11, par 1. (Monti, 250).

[36] *Breviloquium*, Part 4, Ch 11, par 3 (Monti, 251).

[37] *Breviloquium*, Part 6, Ch 11, par 3 (Monti 251-52).

[38] *Breviloquium*, Part 6, Ch 11, par 3 (Monti, 252).

body through which "the soul contracts spiritual diseases." Regarding the reception of the sacrament, Bonaventure maintains that it too must be determined by its end, "which is to make our passage to heaven more rapid through the unburdening of venial sin and the turning our mind to God."[39] It is instructive that it is only within this context of the sacrament that Bonaventure talks about the prolongation of life, suggesting that "it is expedient that [by means of the sacrament of Extreme Unction] many of those who are sick should live longer in order to increase their merit."[40] The only reason for prolonging life is to help the person prepare more fully for the life to come. Thus care for the dying therefore is not seen in terms of prolonging life but in preparing the person for a holy death. The person remains a pilgrim, even as he or she confronts the glory and the anguish that is death.

St. Bernardine of Siena

At this point it might be helpful to move from our intellectual tradition to the Franciscan tradition of popular preaching in the Middle Ages and say something about the sermons of St. Bernardine of Siena, living in the fifteenth century. He was one of the most famous preachers of his day. Today we might even call him a celebrity. In the towns where he preached, people – from the learned and powerful to those minimally lettered – would listen to his peaching, often for up to three hours at a time.[41] Although he predates the tradition of the *Ars moriendi*, Bernardine nevertheless devoted at least thirty of his sermons and treatises to the subject of the "Last Things."[42] One reason for this might be that, unlike Bonaventure, Bernardine was addressing audi-

---

[39] *Breviloquium*, Part 6, Ch 11, par 5 (Monti, 253).

[40] *Breviloquium*, Part 6, Ch 11, par 3 (Monti, 252).

[41] See Franco Mormando, *The Preacher's Demons: Bernardino of Siena and the Social Underworld of Early Renaissance Italy* (Chicago: University of Chicago Press, 1999), 1-12.

[42] Franco Mormando, "What Happens to Us When We Die? Bernardino of Siena on 'The Four Last Things,'" in DuBruck and Gusick, eds., *Death and Dying in the Middle Ages*, 110.

ences in the cities and towns that had been devastated by the Plague[43] and who saw themselves as living constantly in the shadow of death. He would remind his congregations that "constant meditation upon death and its aftermath is a necessary and salutary exercise to Christians who want to save their souls."[44] He described death as "inevitably bitter for all of human kind 'due to our natural condition,'" but for the righteous it was also a "release from prison, the end of exile, the termination of life's hard labor, the departure from a ruined house, an escape from all the perils of life, a return to the homeland, the beginning of life, and the entry to eternal glory."[45] Even so, it remained an ambivalent event even for the righteous. For sinners, however, it was "unremediably horrible,"[46] filled with bodily suffering and mental anguish. In his sermon *De duodecem doloribus quos patitur peccator in hora mortis*, he was quite graphic in his descriptions of this suffering. He described the first affliction of the dying sinner as follows:

> His head feels pain; his body feels pain; his arms feel pain; all of his external and internal body parts feel pain. Nearby stand his wife, family, doctors, and a whole crowd of relatives. One consoles him, another expresses hope of his recovering health. Still another orders medicine, another gives him syrups, yet another puts on a plaster. They rub his body to soothe him, and they pour rose water on his hands and on his feet to bring some relief to them. And, despite all of this,

---

[43] Mormando, "What Happens to Us When We Die?" 109.

[44] Mormando, "What Happens to Us When We Die?" 110.

[45] Mormando, "What Happens to Us When We Die?" 111. Mormando is quoting from the sermon of the Friday after the First Sunday of Lent, *De duodecim doloribus quos patitur peccator in hora mortis. Opera omnia*, Volume 1, 160. One can see similarities between this understanding and Bonaventure's notion of death as transitus.

[46] Mormando, "What Happens to Us When We Die?" 112.

the pain just grows stronger, his body torments him, he wails, he laments: Heu, hai, hei, hem, hem, hem![47]

Soon the devil will come to lead the person to judgment. Describing this fourth affliction, Bernardine mimics the devil:

"Come, O wretched one, to appear before God." Oh what terror, what horror, what astonishment when the wretched soul sees these demons prepared to pounce on their prey! O foolish soul, who will protect you in the hour of such great need? Who will console you? Who will stand by you?[48]

It is within this context of mental anguish that Franco Mormando discusses Bernardine's belief that clinging to life and "the foolish belief that one can evade death" demonstrate an attachment to a life that is still "sinfully loved."[49]

Comparing Bonaventure and Bernardine, one can see an interesting contrast between them. Like Bonaventure, Bernardine speaks of death as the separation of the soul and body, and like Bonaventure, he sees this as part of the anguish and suffering of the dying. But while for Bonaventure this speaks of an appropriate desire that soul and body have for the other that will not be satisfied until the resurrection of the body, this separation is understood very differently by Bernardine. Because the sinner clings to things of this world, it is for this reason that the separation of the soul from the body is especially painful for the sinner.[50] Furthermore, given this suffering and pain, the one who is attached to this life may be unable even to make a proper act of contrition. Ber-

---

[47] Bernardine of Siena, *De duodecim doloribus quos patitur peccator in hora mortis. Opera omnia*, Volume 1, 156.

[48] Bernardine of Siena, "*De duedecim doloribus*," 1, 162.

[49] Mormando, "What Happens to Us When We Die?" 112.

[50] Mormando, "What Happens to Us When We Die?" 113. See "*De duodecim doloribus*," 1, 160.

nardine concludes that "it is difficult and almost impossible for the soul to escape and be saved."[51]

DEATH AND DYING IN CONTEMPORARY MEDICINE

The questions regarding death and dying that concerned the Franciscan intellectual tradition might seem quaint to us today. They seem so foreign to what most of us in this room feel as the real questions that theology and medical ethics need to face in this morally complex world of the twenty-first century. May I suggest that our contemporary attitude is the result of an unprecedented century of growth in medicine and medical technology. Medical technology has expanded our understanding of medical pathologies and our ability to treat them. Technology has also changed our understanding of the very nature of sickness and death themselves. We no longer see sickness as controlling us but rather as something that we can and ought to control. Prolonging life is no longer seen as a taboo but often as an obligation.

As I was preparing this lecture, I received a phone call from a medical center to which I often give ethical advice. A ninety-four year old woman had been admitted from a nursing home. She was diagnosed with end-stage dementia and had not been verbal since 2005. She was experiencing progressive physical deterioration, including serial cardiac arrests, respiratory failure, heart failure, kidney failure, and septic shock. The clinical recommendation was comfort care and hospice, but her son demanded that everything possible be done to keep his mother alive, a choice which is acceptable according to the statutory form of the Illinois Durable Power of Attorney for Health Care. He believed that because medicine was able to keep his mother alive physicians ought to do so.

The philosopher Daniel Callahan, founder of the Hastings Center, a major bioethics think tank, has addressed this contemporary phenomenon:

---

[51] Mormando, "What Happens to Us When We Die?" Mormando is quoting from "*De duodecim doloribus*," 1, 141.

The use of technology is ordinarily the way, in modern medicine, that action is carried out: to give a pill, to cut out a cancerous tumor, or to use a machine to support respiration. With an ethos of technological monism, all meaningful actions ... are technological, whether technological acts or technological omissions. What nature does, its underlying natural causes and pathologies, becomes irrelevant. No death is "natural" any longer – the word becomes meaningless – no natural cause necessarily determinative, no pathology fatal unless failure to deploy a technology makes it so.[52]

Technological monism, this belief that all meaningful actions are technological, can in turn lead to what Callahan calls technological brinkmanship, "pushing aggressive treatment as far as it can go in the hope that it can be stopped at just the right moment if it turns out to be futile."[53]

Unfortunately, even today medicine lacks the precision necessary for such brinkmanship to succeed. Lines become more and more blurred. Physicians continue to pursue aggressive treatment aimed at prolonging life for their patients beyond any reasonable hope for success either because they fear lawsuits from family members such as the one I mentioned above or because, once they have begun a course of action, they simply do not know when or how to stop. Patients themselves begin fearing not only dying, but especially an impersonal death surrounded by tubes, wires, and machines. Some patients have even begun to view all such technologies as oppressive, robbing them of their dignity. They tell relatives that they do not want to be kept alive "on tubes." Yet they also fear refusing such treatments, believing that to be an indication that they are now "hopeless" cases. They fear that others will no longer respond to their real medical

---

[52] Daniel Callahan, *The Troubled Dream of Life: In Search of a Peaceful Death* (Washington, DC: Georgetown University Press, 2000), 68.

[53] Callahan, *The Troubled Dream of Life*, 192. See also 40-42.

and emotional needs. They fear death and they equally fear abandonment while still living. Medical technology, with its promise of prolonged life and human flourishing, thus can become a threat to such flourishing.

Euthanasia and Assisted Suicide

It is this cycle of expectation and disappointment in technology that has in part led to an increasing acceptance of euthanasia and assisted suicide in many countries around the world. Such attitudes are understandable, especially when such disappointment is linked with advocacy of patient autonomy. Although respect for such autonomy has been a supporting pillar of contemporary medical ethics, several writers have begun to criticize what they consider an exaggeration of autonomy.[54] Fifteen years ago, the bioethicist Arthur Caplan suggested that "the preeminence of autonomy reflects the fact that there is no broad consensus as to what constitutes good or bad with respect to the aims of health care."[55] The situation is no different today.

This lack of consensus regarding the good and its resultant stress on individual autonomy in turn have led to what Carl Schneider has termed the model of consumer choice in health care.[56] Briefly described, this notion presupposes that health-care consumers, as all consumers, should be able to choose the kinds of products they prefer. The model then "seeks to allow customers to make successful choices providing them with a market that works ... efficiently."[57] When one combines this notion of consumer choice with the less than successful results of medical brinkmanship, it becomes understandable why many would see euthanasia as a plausible alternative. It becomes simply another choice among the "full

---

[54] See, for example, Willard Gaylin and Bruce Jennings, *The Perversion of Autonomy* (New York: The Free Press, 1996).

[55] Arthur L. Caplan, *If I Were a Rich Man Could I Buy a Pancreas?* (Bloomington: Indiana University Press, 1992), 256.

[56] Carl E. Schneider, "From Consumer Choice to Consumer Welfare," *Hastings Center Report* 25, no. 6 (November-December 1995): S25.

[57] Schneider, "From Consumer Choice to Consumer Welfare."

range of choices" that are offered to the consumer. This understanding has become widely accepted within the United States, from Oregon's Death with Dignity Act legalizing assisted suicide to the writings and political action of physicians such as Timothy Quill.[58] Within the Catholic theological community, it is also becoming accepted by some such as Dick Westley[59] and Hans Küng.[60]

If no death is really natural and if all meaningful actions are technological, there then can be no real distinction between omission and commission. In the face of suffering then it can easily seem more compassionate to accept a patient's choice to hasten death rather than to cause continued suffering. Since ending such suffering lies within human control, it therefore seems that not to use such means would be immoral. As already mentioned, this reaction avoids important questions of the human good. It offers no room for perspectives of reverence for life or for humility before God, attitudes which have long been guides for both moral theology in general and for the Franciscan intellectual tradition.

Medical Vitalism

A variety of medical ethicists, alarmed by this growing trend toward the legalization of euthanasia and assisted suicide, have begun to defend an opposite extreme, what has come to be called medical vitalism. This can be described as those attempts to preserve physical life in and of itself without any significant hope for the recovery of the patient.[61] Consider the following statement of the Catholic moralist,

---

[58] See Timothy Quill, *A Midwife Through the Dying Process* (Baltimore: The Johns Hopkins University Press, 1996). See also Timothy Quill and Margaret Battin, eds., *Physician-Assisted Dying: The Case for Palliative Care and Patient Choice* (Baltimore: The Johns Hopkins University Press, 2004).

[59] Dick Westley, *When It's Right to Die: Conflicting Voices, Difficult Choices* (Mystic, Connecticut: Twenty-Third Publications, 1995).

[60] Hans Küng and Walter Jens, *Dying with Dignity: A Plea for Personal Responsibility* (New York: Continuum Publishing Company, 1996).

[61] See, for example, Richard A. McCormick, *Health and Medicine in the Catholic Tradition* (New York: Crossroad, 1984), 54.

Germain Grisez: "Acts which effect nothing more than keeping a person alive, no matter what that person's condition, do really benefit the person, even if only in a small way, and so, if not done for some ulterior reason, do express love toward the person."[62] The language used here is illustrative. Prolonging life necessarily benefits a patient and therefore should be seen as an act of love. The implication is that any withdrawal of such life-sustaining treatment is morally suspect. The current debate about medically assisted nutrition and hydration, especially for permanently unconscious patients, also has much to say about this perspective.[63]

In our present social context, with so much pressure to legalize euthanasia, it is not difficult to understand the motivation behind medical vitalism. However, such an understanding, no matter how well motivated by fear of euthanasia, also reads our moral tradition through the lens of technological monism. By doing so, it simplifies rather than clarifies our tradition. Furthermore, it demands the acceptance of the same premises as those articulated by the supporters of euthanasia: It is not disease which causes death but rather the physician's or patient's refusal to use the means available to prolong life. No death is natural; all meaningful actions are technological. Most ironically, in view of our Catholic moral tradition, such reasoning increases the likelihood of technological brinkmanship and further dissatisfaction. Callahan expresses the dilemma in the following way:

> Thus was created the perfect double bind: If you are serious about the value of life and the evil of death, you must not stand in the way of medical science, our

---

[62] Germain Grisez, "Should Nutrition and Hydration Be Provided to Permanently Comatose and Other Mentally Disabled Persons?" *Linacre Quarterly* 57 (May 1990): 38.

[63] See Ronand P. Hamel and James J. Walter, eds., *Artificial Nutrition and Hydration and the Permanently Unconscious Patient* (Washington, DC: Georgetown University Press, 2007). See also Congregation for the Doctrine of the Faith, "Responses to Certain Questions Concerning Artificial Nutrition and Hydration and Commentary," *Origins* 37, 17 (September 17, 2007): 241-45.

best hope to eliminate it. If you hesitate to use that science to its fullest, to give it every benefit of doubt, you are convicted not only of failure of hope for the efficacy of science, but also of a lack of seriousness about the sanctity of life.[64]

This seems to be the dilemma that contemporary Christians who are serious about their ethical responsibilities at the end of life seem to face. Does the Franciscan intellectual tradition have anything to say to them?

A DIALOGUE BETWEEN THE FRANCISCAN INTELLECTUAL TRADITION AND CONTEMPORARY MEDICINE

This final section will be more evocative than definitive. Allen Verhey, a Calvinist moral theologian and medical ethicist, tells a story about a conversation with his son who at the time was in the second grade. His son had asked him what he did for a living. His response was that he was a theologian. This gave rise to a second question, "What do theologians do?" Verhey's response was that they talk of God. His son then asked a third question: "With who?" Years later, as Verhey reflected on that third question, he finally found an answer: "Theologians talk of God with any who will. Indeed sometimes they may and must talk of God with some who would rather not."[65] I believe that the Franciscan intellectual tradition must likewise enter into dialogue regarding end of life care with those who will and also with those who would rather not enter such a dialogue. Members of both of these groups will be found both not only outside of the Church but inside as well.

What can the Franciscan tradition say? I would like to explore very briefly three possible areas where the dialogue between the Franciscan intellectual tradition and contem-

---

[64] Callahan, 86.

[65] Allen Verhey, *Reading the Bible in the Strange World of Medicine* (Grand Rapids, Michigan: William B. Eerdmans Publishing Company, 2003), 23.

porary medicine might be fruitful: 1) a retrieval of the moral tradition of ordinary/extraordinary means as a response to the increasing technologizing of end of life care, 2) a similar retrieval of how an understanding of the afterlife affects the understanding of end of life care itself, and 3) a return to a fuller understanding of the meaning and importance of the Catholic/Christian tradition of care itself.

The "Ordinary/Extraordinary Means" Tradition

Since the sixteenth century, Catholic practice regarding the prolongation of life has been guided by the distinction between "ordinary" and "extraordinary" means.[66] This distinction has been succinctly described in the United States Conference of Catholic Bishops' Ethical and Religious Directives for Catholic Health Care Services:

> A person may forgo extraordinary or disproportionate means of preserving life. Disproportionate means are those that in the patient's judgment do not offer a reasonable hope of benefit or entail an excessive burden, or impose excessive expense on the family or the community.[67]

Conversely, ordinary means are those which do offer reasonable hope of benefit without entailing an excessive burden, and are therefore considered morally obligatory.

---

[66] Recently, the Vatican has attempted to change the terminology to "proportionate" and "disproportionate," but this attempt has not met with success. See the Congregation for the Doctrine of the Faith, Declaration on Euthanasia (May 5, 1980), Part IV. For a history of the tradition of ordinary and extraordinary means, see Russell E. Smith, ed., *Conserving Human Life* (Boston: Pope John Paul XXIII Medical-Moral Research and Education Center, 1989).

[67] United States Conference of Catholic Bishops, Ethical and Religious Directives for Catholic Health Care Services, Fourth Edition (Washington, DC: U.S.C.C.B., 2001), 31. The directive quoted is Directive #57.

Allowing the Franciscan intellectual tradition to enter into a fuller dialogue with this moral tradition highlights the fact that, as shown earlier in this paper, the latter tradition itself is as dependent upon Francis Bacon and the growth of technology as upon the Catholic moral tradition. It is part of the Catholic Church's continuing questioning of the moral limits of technology. In emphasizing that we are not obliged to use extraordinary or disproportionate means, therefore, the tradition is not denying the good of technology or stating that some lives are not worth living on the other hand. Rather, it is calling upon people to accept the fact that no matter how advanced medical technology is, there will be times when it reaches its limits. The tradition maintains that although preserving life is a good, this does not justify treatment which is excessively burdensome or useless, that does not offer hope of success. This dialogue with the Franciscan intellectual tradition can thus re-emphasize the fact that simply because a procedure is technologically possible does not necessarily mean that the procedure is morally appropriate – this being true even for life-prolonging technologies.

The Theological Understanding of Death

A second element that a conversation between contemporary Christian bioethics and the Franciscan intellectual tradition might emphasize is directed to a deficiency in contemporary bioethics itself. Over the past forty years, Christians have decried the secularization of this field. Allen Verhey, for example has contrasted what he has called and "early and worthy tradition of bioethics" with the contemporary state of affairs. He challenges contemporary Christian bioethicists "to talk candidly about the difference it makes to be a believer, to speak prophetically concerning the culture, and to draw out the implications for bioethics of such faith and criticism."[68]

---

[68] Verhey, 20.

The Franciscan intellectual tradition may have something prophetic to say about returning Christian bioethics to a solidly theological basis. If one looks at the tradition of prolonging life and the ordinary/extraordinary distinction, one does not find anything distinctively Christian or Catholic. Yet, medieval theologians like Bonaventure – and medieval preachers like Bernardine – necessarily began with an explicit theology of death. What would theological bioethics look like today if its practitioners had to articulate such a theology of death and then show how that theology related to their concrete ethical method?

Bonaventure's understanding of death as the separation of the soul from the body had concrete ramifications for his understanding of care of the dying and for his belief concerning the suffering one faces at death. Seldom today are bioethicists challenged to articulate their own theology of death and to explain how that understanding explicitly enters into their assessment of end of life decisions. Perhaps one of the few theologians to explicitly articulate such a theology of death has been Karl Rahner. His theological understanding of the process of dying is directly related to his understanding of transcendental freedom: "Death," he says, "is the breaking in of finality upon mere transience – that finality which is the concretization of freedom come to its maturity."[69] Yet Rahner, himself dying prior to the great movements in bioethics, never articulated how such a theological point of view would affect both the decisions regarding the end of life and the care of the dying person. Understanding a theology of death as a foundation for bioethics may be more important today than ever before.

A Catholic Theology of Care for the Dying

The Catholic ethical tradition regarding the end of life prides itself in being an ethic of care. The Ethical and Reli-

---

[69] Karl Rahner, "On Christian Dying," in *Theological Investigations*, Volume VII: Further Theology of the Spiritual Life (New York: The Seabury Press, 1977), 289.

gious Directives state that the Catholic health care institution "as a witness to faith ... will be a community of respect, love and support to patients or residents and their families as they face the reality of death." The Directives go on to remind physicians that the "task of medicine is to care even when it cannot cure."[70] A conversation between the Franciscan intellectual tradition and Catholic bioethics can, however, clarify the true meaning of care.

Rooted in the Middle Ages, the Franciscan tradition has not been inclined to equate care with the prolongation of life. This has also been part of the genius of the traditional distinction between ordinary and extraordinary means. Yet, as we have seen, the reaction to a perceived threat by the forces desiring legalized euthanasia continues to push many Catholic theologians and even members of the Magisterium to a position closer and closer to medical vitalism. The Franciscan intellectual tradition arose at a time when to prolong life was seen as immoral, and even possibly evidence of an attachment to a life that was still "sinfully loved."[71] The Franciscan intellectual tradition thus raises larger questions regarding the nature and complexity of care for the dying. In a similar way, Richard McCormick has contrasted the "medical good" with what is truly good for a patient.[72] As the trend in Catholic bioethics seems to equate the two, perhaps the Franciscan intellectual tradition can become a source out of which to raise questions regarding what medical interventions – and what end of life care – reflect what is truly good for a terminally ill patient.

CONCLUSION

The "long answer" has taken us quite far from St. Francis's simple embrace of death as a sister "from whom no one

---

[70] *Ethical and Religious Directives*, 29.
[71] See Mormando, "What Happens to Us When We Die?" 112.
[72] Richard A. McCormick, *Health and Medicine in the Catholic Tradition*, 115.

living can escape."[73] Yet, I hope that long and perhaps circuitous route might enable us to understand more fully not
only the Franciscan intellectual tradition on the one hand or
contemporary bioethics on the other but most of all how they
can enter into a fruitful conversation for moral action in a
complex world.

---

[73] St. Francis, "The Canticle of Creatures," *FA:ED* 1, 114.

MORAL DECISION-MAKING AS DISCERNMENT: SCOTUS AND PRUDENCE

MARY BETH INGHAM, C.S.J.

In the three decades since the publication of Carol Gilligan's *In a Different Voice*,[1] feminist writers have developed a sustained critique of contemporary moral philosophy. Ethicists among them argue that the Kantian-Kohlbergian analysis of moral development and decision-making does not accurately reflect women's experience in making moral judgments.[2] The ethical analysis proper to modernity betrays women's moral intuitions and defends a male-dominant paradigm. In response to this feminist critique, some ethicists object to its apparent lack of foundation. They point out that the feminist perspective appears to privilege women's experience in the way the earlier tradition has favored men. The ethics of care promoted by feminist ethicists does not seem able to explain and justify its own conclusions. At times, it resembles a situationist-type theory. Susan Parsons[3] rightly points out that the dominant libertarian moral model may not furnish

---

[1] Carol Gilligan, *In a Different Voice* (Cambridge, MA: Harvard University Press, 1982).

[2] Rita Manning, in her *Speaking from the Heart: A Feminist Perspective on Ethics* (Lanham, MD: Rowman and Littlefield, 1992), offers a very good version of this critique, complete with her own survey illustrating its power. See especially chapter 3, 33-43.

[3] "Feminist Ethics after Modernity: Towards an Appropriate Universalism," *Studies in Christian Ethics*, vol. 8, n. 1, (1995), 77-94.

the best way for feminist ethics to develop and that other alternatives need to be explored.

ELEMENTS OF THE FEMINIST CRITIQUE

The most important dimension of modern ethical discussion critiqued by feminist thinkers is the foundation for the moral order. They reject the Natural Law tradition of the Aristotelian-Thomistic approach as well as the rights/obligational tradition of the Kantian-Rawlsian perspective. In addition, the utilitarian/consequentialist methodology, with its calculus of cost/benefit offers no concern for persons and for the value of relationships. All three classic moral approaches point to an abstract, depersonalized and universal foundation upon which moral decision-making must be based. By contrast, feminist thinkers hold that the true basis for moral judgments is expressed in the way women actually make moral decisions. This refers less to the deduction of norms from a priori principles, but to the affirmation of human connectedness and relationships. For a renewed moral order, one needs a relational and interpersonal foundation.

A second feminist critique points to what is needed for moral decision-making and judgment. Susan Sherwin[4] rightly points to the dangers of abstraction and generalization in Kantian ethics. Rita Manning stresses the importance of the moral context and to the significance of the particularity of each moral decision. For Manning, the so-called "textbook conception" of ethical theory has promoted expectations both of too much and too little. Moral theories are expected to do too much: they must provide answers to virtually every situation. But they are also seen to do too little: they present ethical theories that compete with one another. This inevitably produces moral skepticism. In both cases, contemporary

---

[4] "Feminist and Medical Ethics: Two Different Approaches to Contextual Ethics," *Feminist Perspectives in Medical Ethics*, (Bloomington, IN: Indiana University Press, 1992), 17-31.

moral discussion does not pay sufficient attention to the concrete matter for moral consideration.[5]

This lack of attention to the particular is especially egregious where rule-based moral theories (such as rule-utilitarianism) are concerned. Since rules must be applied impartially, one must disregard the specific aspects of a situation in order to discover the general characteristics. It is these general aspects that allow one to apply the principle or rule correctly. The result of this sort of approach is that rules dominate over particular aspects of a situation. It is a type of "moral reductionism" that plays well in the abstract, but can be horrible in the concrete, where real persons are concerned. Indeed, the moral situation is precisely what it is by virtue of those particular aspects that specify this rather than that. A fully developed moral approach should be able to take into account specific and particular elements of the concrete situation, without falling into relativism or subjectivism.

A third and final critique involves the exclusivity of moral concerns today. Elizabeth Johnson[6] calls for an expanded moral vision, broadened to include the environment. Annette Baier[7] argues that ethics ought to concern itself not only with actions and relationships, but with character formation and the development of attitudes of trust. Finally, Sidney Callahan[8] emphasizes feminine qualities which are essential to good moral action: emotion, intuition, realism and care. A truly human moral approach should be both inclusive of all persons and all situations and be expansive in its possibilities.

All these authors identify the narrowness characteristic of traditional modern ethical discussion. With its foundation in abstract or overly general rules, contemporary moral theories do not promote the good of persons. With their calculus-

---

[5] See her discussion in *Speaking from the Heart*, 20-22.

[6] Elizabeth A. Johnson, *Woman, Earth and Creator Spirit*, (Mahwah, NJ: Paulist Press, 1993).

[7] "Trust and Anti-Trust," *Ethics* 96 (1986): 231-60.

[8] Sidney Callahan, *Good Conscience; Reason and Emotion in Moral Decision Making*, (San Francisco: HarperOne, 1991).

based or deductive approach, they do not offer the flexibility needed to handle situations that fall outside the particular contours of the rules at hand. Finally, they strive toward too much de-personalized thinking, overlooking character formation, the role of emotions and the value of relationships. Too often ethics takes as its focus extraordinarily odd situations, such as fat people trapped in caves or babies tied to railroad tracks. These situations are not only ones of extreme violence, but they are also so outlandish that no one could ever possibly imagine them as real life situations for moral decisions. In this case, how then do they serve any function other than to hone the analytic skills of those involved in classroom discussion?

These questions and concerns guide our reflection. What I would like to do is to take seriously this contemporary feminist critique of modern moral models and offer, as a helpful remedy, the thought of Franciscan John Duns Scotus. With his aesthetic model for moral goodness, Scotus elaborates a theory of moral decision-making that is more akin to artistic practice than to mathematical deduction. Moral situations appear as opportunities for creativity and beauty, as moments when the moral agent acts as a creative artist. Moral wisdom, known as prudence, functions within this vision as a type of artistic discernment. The moral agent "sees" something in the present situation that calls forth her creative response. The result of this "moral vision" is the birthing of goodness, relationship and life in the particular set of circumstances at hand. In this way, Scotus's approach to moral-decision making may provide what is needed for a renewed moral discussion today: a moral foundation based on love and beauty, moral judgment as a discerning of goodness and beauty, and moral action as giving birth to beauty, in the agent and in the world.

My presentation has three parts. In the first, I briefly recall the significant moral elements of Scotus vision, highlighting what they mean for prudence or moral wisdom. In the second, we put theory into practice, with a moral situation for analysis. Finally, in the third concluding section,

I highlight five elements of moral discernment that Scotus would advocate.

A. *The contours of Scotus's moral vision*

The first significant element is the nature of moral goodness. In *Ordinatio* I, D. 17, Prima Pars, q. 2, Scotus compares moral goodness to harmony. Like beauty, goodness is the integration of all conditions necessary for an act to be whole or complete. Moral goodness decorates the act, "including a combination of due proportion to all to which it [the act] should be proportioned (such as potency, object, end, time, place, and manner), and this especially as right reason dictates...."[9] Moral perfection involves the ability to choose and act in such a way that all particular conditions are in harmony with one another and with the demands of reason. The fulfillment of moral excellence is the proper interaction of the science and craft of prudence in the act of moral deliberation and choice.

In his Quodlibetal Question 18, Scotus returns to this aesthetic approach when he defines the morally good act as "having all that the agent's right reason declares must pertain to the act or the agent in acting."[10] The morally good act is one which balances the good of action, place, timing, manner, creating a "whole" that is integrated and harmonious. Moral goodness is suitable to the situation and to the person.

True moral maturity involves both internal harmony and external beauty. A morally good act is both suitable for an individual to perform and has its own coherence or suitability. This suitability involves three foundational elements: namely, the nature of the agent, the nature of the act and the power by which the agent does what she does. A first moral judgment involves these questions: Who am I? What am I doing? Scotus states that, on the basis of these questions, one

---

[9] *Ordinatio* I, d. 17, n. 62 (Vatican V, 163-64).

[10] In *God and Creatures: The Quodlibetal Questions*, Felix Alluntis and Allan B. Wolter, O.F.M. (Princeton, NJ: Princeton University Press: 1975), n. 18.8, 400.

can make the first moral determination needed in a given situation. This determination involves the action understood as object for moral consideration. The first question, "who am I?" takes into account personal identity as well as integrity of character. The second question, "what am I doing?" looks at the action insofar as it expresses my own identity, or (in the case of a vicious act) betrays who I am. Scotus argues that everyone knows who they are and what they are doing. These two questions form the moral foundation for any situation.

Moral goodness has a natural dimension, and this, too, is likened to beauty by Scotus.

> I say that natural goodness is like beauty of body, which results from a combination of all that is internally harmonious and is becoming to the body, such as size, color, and figure (as Augustine wants to say of a good face in Book VIII of *The Trinity*: "Good is the face of a man with regular features, a cheerful expression, and a glowing color.") And this natural goodness is not that which is coextensive with being, but that which is opposed to evil and is a second perfection of a thing, in which we find united all that is becoming to it and is internally harmonious.[11]

Natural beauty is the foundation upon which moral beauty depends. An act which has no natural beauty cannot have moral beauty. In his own aesthetic moral approach, Scotus build levels of beauty upon levels of beauty, beginning with the most foundational natural harmony that the initial act possesses. Significant in this first level is that Scotus clarifies that this goodness is not that metaphysical goodness that is coextensive with being. Rather, it is that foundational level of goodness whose opposite is evil and is, as he clarifies "a second perfection." This second perfection is beyond the goodness of mere existence, it involves the internal harmony and

---

[11] *Ordinatio* II, d. 40. English from Allan B. Wolter, *Duns Scotus on the Will and Morality* (Washington: CUA Press, 1997), 176. All references will be to this later edition, edited by William Frank.

integrity of an act. It is the first dimension upon which moral goodness depends.

Following upon this, additional moral aspects involve the end for which the act is performed, the manner in which one performs the act, the timing of the act and its place. To be perfectly good, "an act must be faultless on all counts."[12] All aspects of the situation must be present and appropriately so. The appropriate moral judgment required for such a determination belongs to prudence, right reasoning. Acts lacking in the fullness of perfection can be either privatively or positively bad. Privative badness occurs where one of the minor characteristics is missing. One might tell the truth in a given situation, but at the wrong time. One might give to the poor, but grudgingly. Positive badness occurs where a central characteristic is missing or disordered. For example, one might tell the truth to someone in order to hurt them, or give someone bad news with glee. In these two examples, the disorder has to do with the intention to give pain to another. The actions are in some sense ugly. They are vicious.

The better the act is, the more levels of beauty it possesses. Scotus uses the example of going to church. He identifies several dimensions of goodness, each corresponding to a different dictate of right reason or prudence.

> For example, I go to church to fulfill an obligation in justice, because of obedience to some vow. And I also go out of charity or love for God, to pray or to worship him. And I also go out of fraternal charity to edify my neighbor. In short, the more morally good motives there are, the better the act is.[13]

Because he frames his moral discussion around the context of beauty, Scotus exemplifies that tradition of medieval thinkers who bring spirituality into their moral discussion. Moral decisions do not belong to a separate or isolated dimension of human life. They are not the domain of class-

---

[12] Quodlibetal Question 18, n. 18.16 (*God and Creatures*, 404)

[13] Quodlibetal Question 18, n. 18.22 (*God and Creatures*, 405-06).

room discussion, of problem-solving techniques. Rather, they manifest the totality of the human rational, spiritual journey. Moral actions are not simply a subset of that narrow category of dilemmas: they are part of everyday life.

The focus on internal harmony naturally points to Scotus's depiction of the moral agent as functioning morally by means of the two Anselmian affections. Recall that Anselm, in his discussion of rational willing, identified two metaphysical orientations within the will. The first is the natural *affectio commodi*, the deep desire for happiness and security within every living being. The second, more proper to rational beings, is the *affectio iustitiae*, or the affection for justice. Here is the free and rational desire we possess. It is the affection for justice that draws us toward integrity and honor, it inspires us to search for goods of lasting value, this affection enables us to control our other desires and, where needed, offer a counter-weight to the affection for happiness. Alexander of Hales, writing at the beginning of thirteenth century, had identified intrinsic values (*honestatem*) as "intelligible beauty."[14] Goods of this type are the object of the affection for justice. In this way we see how, even within the tradition, the human metaphysical desire for the higher goods is identified with the desire for beauty.

But the affection for justice is not simply a desire for intelligible beauty. Scotus calls it the "checkrein" on the affection for happiness.

> Therefore, this affection for justice, which is the first checkrein on the affection for the beneficial, inasmuch as we need not actually seek that towards which the latter affection inclines us, nor must we seek it above all else (namely, to the extent to which we are inclined by this affection for the advantageous) – this affection for what is just, I say, is the liberty innate to the will,

---

[14] Alexander of Hales, *Summa Theologica* I, 3, 3, n. 103 (Quarrachi: Ad Claras Aquas, 1924), Vol. I, 162: *Cum bonum dicatur dupliciter, honestum et utile…. Honestatem autem voco intelligibilem pulchritudinem, quam nos spiritualem proprie dicimus….*

since it represents the first checkrein on this affection for the advantageous.[15]

This higher affection is rational and free; it constitutes the moral domain and distinguishes us from the animal kingdom. According to Scotus (and Anselm, for that matter), moral action would be impossible without both affections, balanced in an internal harmony of desire. The interaction of these two affections offers the metaphysical constitution of freedom as self-mastery: the ability of the person to wait before acting.

A third element is the activity of intellection. Here Scotus offers two acts of human cognitive power that help us understand what goes on in the moral situation. These acts are those of abstraction and intuition. In the act of abstraction, the mind generalizes from the specific to the more general in order to understand reality according to shared qualities. The act of intuition, on the other hand, grasps the singular in the concrete reality of its existence. In his *Lectura*, Book II, distinction 3, Scotus describes the act of intuition as distinct from the act of abstraction in the following manner:

> Know that an intellect is capable of two sorts of knowledge and intellection, for it can have one that abstracts from all existence, and another of a thing present in its own existence ... The first sort of knowledge, according to which the intellect abstracts from all existence, is called "abstractive," whereas the other, according to which the intellect sees the thing in its existence, is called "intuitive." It is not called "intuitive" because it is not discursive, however, but rather because it is distinguished from that abstractive knowledge, which knows a thing in itself through a species.[16]

---

[15] *Ordinatio* II, d. 6. English from *Will and Morality*, 1997, 298-99.

[16] English translation from Allan Wolter, "Intuition, Memory and Our knowledge of Individuals," *The Philosophical Theology of John Duns Sco-*

Both Sebastian Day[17] and Allan Wolter[18] maintain that intuition includes all that abstraction does, along with the certainty coming from the cognitive immediacy. This suggests that intuition is a more foundational rational act than abstraction, and is itself the grounding for abstraction.

We know that Scotus developed his cognitional theory against the Aristotelian framework of the Posterior Analytics and the identification of scientific knowledge with abstract, universal propositions presented in syllogistic form. Interesting for the present discussion is that, in his *De Primo Principio*, Scotus identifies intuition as the superior mental act.

Knowledge through what is similar is merely knowledge under a universal aspect, to the extent that the things are alike. Through such a universal what properly distinguishes each would remain unknown. Furthermore, such a knowledge through a universal is not intuitive but abstractive, and intuitive knowledge is the more perfect of the two.[19]

While abstractive cognition is proper to scientific reflection and therefore to moral science as an intermediate category between principles and actions, intuitive cognition reaches the object precisely in itself and in the act of existence. Richard Dumont points here to the distinguishing characteristic between Scotist and Kantian theories of cognition.[20]

---

tus, Marilyn McCord Adams, ed., (Ithaca, NY: Cornell University Press, 1990), 107.

[17] *Intuitive Cognition: A Key to the Significance of Later Scholastics*, (St. Bonaventure, NY: The Franciscan Institute, 1947).

[18] "The Formal Distinction" in *John Duns Scotus 1265-1965*, John K. Ryan, Bernardino M. Bonansea, eds., (Washington: CUA Press, 1965), 58, reprinted in *The Philosophical Theology of John Duns Scotus*, Marilyn McCord Adams, ed., (Princeton, NJ: Princeton University Press, 1992), 39.

[19] *A Treatise on God as First Principle* (*De Primo Principio*), Allan B. Wolter, Translator and Editor, (Chicago: Franciscan Herald Press, 1966), 149.

[20] "Intuition: Prescript of Postscript to Scotus's Demonstration of God's Existence," in *Deus et Homo ad mentem I. Duns Scoti*, Studia Scholastico-

This means that, in making moral decisions, human reason (according to Scotus) has access both to abstract and general moral norms (which are themselves verified by experience) but also more importantly, to the concrete moral situation in all its particularity. Moral conclusions about what one ought to do must take seriously the contingent situation for choice without dismissing abstract/general moral considerations.

In his presentation of prudence, or moral wisdom, Scotus uses a similar distinction between moral science as abstract and prudence as immediate to choice. He defines prudence as "a habit more immediately directed towards practice, so that a prudent person knows immediately the means to use and does not have to reason backwards from principles to other prior principles."[21] Like geometry, moral science forms a body of deductive truths which exist in God and which can be verified in experience. Reflection upon concrete choices, however, reveals that moral wisdom is organic: prudence is generated at the moment a first right choice is made, and developed through moral training. It is expressed by the fully formed moral agent as "immediate knowledge of what should be done." Like the trained artisan, the morally mature know what to do as they immediately grasp the moral demands of a given situation as a whole. Like the trained musician, the morally mature person "hears" the harmonious interconnection of all moral elements. Here is a type of sophisticated moral intuition that both resembles an aesthetic judgment and is the result of years of living and training.

Finally, the goal of all moral action is mutuality and relationship. Just as the morally good act is beautiful because it involves the harmonious integration of several dimensions, so too the morally good agent possesses the beauty of integration of character. The moral community is built up and founded upon the harmony of relationship and connectedness. Scotus presents divine Triune communion as the ideal

---

Scotistica V (Rome: Societas Internationalis Scotistica, 1972), 86: "Whereas Kant simply denies to the human intellect an intuitive access to reality, Scotus does not."

[21] *Lectura* Prologue. English from *Will and Morality*, 134.

for human society. He personalizes the moral domain when he identifies the first principle of praxis as love for God alone. In this way, he affirms the objectivity of love and the centrality of an *ordo amoris*. This personalized moral domain has implications for his discussion of Natural Law and the requirements of moral living. As we know, Scotus divides the commands of Natural Law (the Decalogue) into two parts: those dealing directly with God and those dealing with the neighbor. Contrary to Aquinas and others of the tradition, Scotus holds that the commands dealing with the neighbor do not belong to Natural Law strictly speaking. Rather, they stand in harmonious relationship to the first command and function as God's desire for human living. In other words, we are perfected relationally by living according to the commands of the second table. This relational perfection involves both the neighbor and God.

Scotus identifies the first practical principle with *Deus diligendus est* (God is to be loved). This analytic proposition grounds both the metaphysical and the moral domains; it defines all reality within the context of love. In *Ordinatio* Book III, d. 27 he explains that human reason possesses a natural capacity to recognize this first principle. In other words, every person naturally possesses the ability to love God above all things and for God alone.

> I say that to love God above all is an act conformed to natural right reason, which dictates that what is best must be loved most; and hence such an act is right of itself. Indeed, as a first practical principle of action, this is something known per se, and hence its rectitude is self-evident.[22]

This rational capacity to love God plays in harmony with the affection for justice. Our deepest natural desire to love the good for its own sake reveals the extent to which the human heart (that is, the center of our rational being) echoes the di-

---

[22] English from *Will and Morality*, 276.

vine heart (the ground for all that exists). The connaturality between our heart and God's heart enables Scotus to draw out the implications of an aesthetic vision without losing the metaphysical and moral foundations that would be needed to avoid subjectivism or relativism. God's loving nature grounds all moral decisions because God's love constitutes beings as they exist. The *ordo amoris* is not an order of human loving, but an order of God's love. Otherwise, moral decisions would fall into the realm of human preference. Consequently, excellent moral decisions seek to imitate the divine heart and divine love for beauty.

In affirming the first principle of love, Scotus confirms the scientific character of charity. He presents the moral domain as one framed in love and, therefore, in beauty. Because he grounds his ethical discussion on the rational will rather than the intellect, he focuses on love as the main content of the moral law and as the only manner by which the law can be fulfilled. Moral living involves both the content and manner of loving. Here means and end coincide. Charity reveals the unity of moral life; joy reveals the heart of moral perfection.

Scotus presents prudence not merely as an isolated virtue, but as the *prudens* or prudent person, one capable of moral insight and intuition, one capable of appreciating moral beauty and bringing it to birth. At all levels of his moral vision, we find a personalized moral domain, calling forth persons, caring for persons, bringing persons to life and health. He speaks of prudence as that important cardinal virtue which is developed over time and within a community supportive of moral goodness.[23] Beyond this, prudence is also a gift of the Spirit, and here prudence is counsel.[24] In a key text, *Ordinatio* III, d. 36, Scotus argues in addition that pru-

---

[23] *Ordinatio* III, d. 34 in *Will and Morality*, 241: "Where creatures are concerned ... the intellect is perfected most perfectly by prudence, if that virtue is most perfect. For then one would have the most perfect practical knowledge about every possible action and under every possible circumstance."

[24] *Ordinatio* III, d. 34 in *Will and Morality*, 249: "Hence the habit whereby someone is counseled is prudence."

dence is *recta ratio*, a scientific capacity containing the first principles of praxis.[25] As a result of these three activities that belong to prudence (first principles, counsel and immediate judgment) we see the manifold activity of prudence as a scientific *habitus* of what should be done. In other words, prudence for Scotus (like Aristotle) is the *prudens*, the morally wise person who knows how to act in any set of circumstances. The domain of prudence lies precisely at the intersection of immediate insight, learned habits, reasoned conclusions and foundational moral principle.

For its most effective functioning, prudential rationality makes use of intuition of particulars and generalizations on the basis of common experiences, of deductive processes belonging to moral science and of attention to the specifics in a concrete decision. In this way, prudence joins together three important realms: foundational moral principles, conclusions based upon scientific reflection and the immediate artistic judgment in a given set of circumstances.

Early in his career, Scotus presents the prudent person as a moral expert who, like the craftsperson, functions as master of the trade.[26] One who is prudent knows immediately what to do in a situation "without having to reason backwards to prior principles." Scotus likens this person to one who "knows how to do or make something" simply from experience. Here again, the immediacy of moral knowledge is what distinguishes prudence from the purely theoretical dimension of moral science. One who knows from experience is immediately active and proximately practical.

---

[25] *Ordinatio* III, d. 36 in *Will and Morality*, 268: "Therefore, it seems that prudence should not be restricted solely to the habit for dictating the specific means which are ordered to a particular chosen end, but should also be concerned with that end properly and per se."

[26] *Lectura* Prologue in *Will and Morality*, 134-35: "Hence, just as an artist with a knowledge of his art in mind is more remotely practical than one who knows [how to do or make something] simply from experience and not deductively from any art he possesses, so too one who knows the science of morals is more remotely practical than one who possesses prudence."

The life of rational and moral excellence results from training and experience. Once prudence is generated, the interaction of the will's two affections continues the process of moral development. The will's capacity for self-control supports and contributes to increased moral excellence as the individual develops a greater and greater ability to make ordered choices. Such moral development is largely dependent upon experience in the concrete act of decision-making, and cannot occur solely on a theoretical level.

Prudence participates in both inductive and deductive domains of reasoning. There is both a science of moral reasoning as well as a craft for moral decisions. The moral realm is defined not only by general principles and norms, but also by rational action and decision within a concrete and particular situation. Prudence is a human craft, learned from experiences, but ultimately rational in its general intent. Principles are helpful but incomplete; universal norms are imperfect. The moral person develops rationally within a society where right appetite is fostered and supported by laws and customs. Perfect and complete moral reasoning can only occur in the concrete particular act of moral decision-making.

As we begin to piece together Scotus's moral perspective, some elements point to and reveal prudence as a type of moral discernment. First, the morally mature person is self-aware: she is conscious of her desires and her moral attractions, she balances her self-related needs against the needs of others. She knows when she can hold back her own desires in favor of the needs of others, or the needs of integrity in a given situation. Second, this person is attentive to the present demands of the given situation. She knows what to look for in the moral equation, she can tell the difference between morally significant and morally insignificant aspects, between details that are irrelevant and those that make the moral situation what it is. She can balance what she sees with the domain of moral principles. She is also attentive to persons within the situation. She is alert to the good that can be done in a given setting, especially in a situation where the raw material for beauty is not all she would hope for.

This bringing together of principles, acquired skill, the deepest rational desires and the particular situation is truly an example of moral discernment. All that is needed is the power of the Spirit of God. This refers to the Spirit's "now," the moment when rational freedom flows forth into creativity, and beauty is brought into the created order.

A. A Case to Consider: Diane and her illness

Against this background of Scotus's moral vision, let us now consider a particular case of moral decision-making. This case is taken from Dr. Timothy Quill's experience dealing with a woman dying of leukemia, and appeared in an article in the 1991 *New England Journal of Medicine* on death and dignity.[27]

Diane was diagnosed with leukemia at a relatively young age. She had been raised in an alcoholic family and had led an isolated life. As a young woman, she had vaginal cancer, and through much of her life had struggled with depression and alcoholism. As she gradually took control of her life, she developed a strong sense of independence and personal confidence. She was sober now, had deeper connections with her husband, son and friends. At the time of the diagnosis, things seemed to be going well.

Dr. Quill's diagnosis sent Diane into a tailspin. When the bone-marrow biopsy confirmed acute myelomonocytic leukemia, the oncologist broke the news to Diane, hoping to spur her to immediate action. Technological advances in medicine led to hope: intervention was often successful, with cures in 25% of the cases. The oncologist hoped to begin chemotherapy that afternoon. To his surprise, Diane was enraged at his presumption that she would even consider treatment and she was devastated by the diagnosis. All she wanted to do was return home to be with her family; she had already decided that she would forgo treatment.

---

[27] "Death and dignity: A Case of Individualized Decision Making," *New England Journal of Medicine*, 324.10 (March 7, 1991): 691-94. Excerpts of this article appeared in a Los Angeles Times Opinion section.

As her husband and family attempted to reason with her, Diane became clear that she did not want any treatment, that she would probably die during the treatment and that the suffering involved in chemotherapy would outweigh the slightly longer period of time she would have with them. Her quality of life would suffer as a result of the treatment. In her opinion, 25% chance of success was not high enough for her to risk the time she had left.

While Dr. Quill was dismayed at her fatalism, he came to understand it and began planning for hospice care. At this moment, Diane surprised him with her desire to maintain control of herself and her own dignity as long as possible. When this was no longer feasible, she wanted to take her own life in "the least painful way possible." Diane's fear of a lingering death would clearly interfere with her ability to enjoy the time remaining. Until she had the assurance of her own ability to end things when she wanted, she knew no peace. Dr. Quill referred her to the Hemlock Society.

The following week, Diane phoned with a request for barbiturates to help her sleep. Dr. Quill knew well that this was the preferred method offered by the Hemlock Society and, while he tried to make sure she was not suffering from depression or in despair, he "wrote the prescription with an uneasy feeling." He also claims that he felt strongly he was "setting her free to get the most out of the time she had left, to maintain dignity and control on her own terms until her death." He met with her regularly for the next few months, but gradually came to see that the time was approaching. They tried to minimize the pain and suffering as best they could, but it was too much for her. She was more terrified of suffering than she was of taking her own life.

The morning she died, Diane said goodbye to her husband and son, and asked them to leave her alone for an hour. When they returned, they found her body on the couch, lying still and covered with a favorite shawl. She appeared peaceful. When they called Dr. Quill, he contacted the medical examiner to report that she had died from "acute leukemia." He did not report the actual cause of death, but only the condition that resulted in death. Quill concludes his story as follows:

> So I said "acute leukemia" to protect all of us, to pro-tect Diane from an invasion into her past and into her body, and to continue to shield society from knowl-edge of the suffering that people often undergo in the process of dying.

What are we to make of this complex situation, in light of the aesthetic moral vision of John Duns Scotus? In such a set of circumstances, what could Diane have done differently? What could Dr. Quill have done differently? What aspects might have promoted something more beautiful than what actually occurred?

In looking at this situation, one following Scotus's ap-proach would highlight the following key aspects. First, her state of mind and heart was one of fear and despair. Clearly, the affection for possession was dominating her decision-making. In addition, she chose isolation from her family in this decision, rather than building up the relationship with them. Rather than allow them to serve and care for her, it was important to her to "retain control as long as possible." Her sense of self depended upon this type of independence, and this type of autonomy.

A second element that Scotus's approach would consid-er involves the options that were identified by her and her doctor. There seem only to be violent courses of action: che-motherapy vs. suicide. Who was advocating for additional alternatives, those which might promote Diane's peace and harmony, her final letting go of the need to control this situ-ation in all its dimensions? Where were the voices seeking to soothe and calm her fears? Might there have been other options, involving her husband, her son and her friends? Sig-nificant in her mode of decision making and action was her desire to "go it alone" and only get help from the one person who could give her what she wanted: the doctor.

While we would certainly look upon Diane with compassion, Dr. Quill seems to fare less well under the Scotist lens. Who was he and what was he doing? A medical professional, he did not act with the integrity of one whose vocation is to promote life. In addition, here was a man who continued to disregard his own emotional state, who continued to assist someone in despair, who continued to do what she asked. His uneasy feelings plagued him throughout, from the first mention of the suicide, to the prescription for the barbiturates, to the falsifying of the medical report. As he states, "The family or I could have been subject to criminal prosecution, and I to professional review, for our roles in support of Diane's choices." "Support for Diane's choices" – this seems to be the way modern moral theories, Kantian or Utilitarian, would have viewed their role in this tragic situation. Diane was the morally mature agent, she was the autonomous person, she had a right to make this choice. Their role was to help her do what she wanted in this matter.

Let us be frank: there is not a great deal of beauty or harmony in this moral scenario. Diane was depressed, the family was helpless, the doctor was weak. For another course of action, perhaps there needed to be a different cast of characters: persons who could lift her up and take appropriate control on her behalf, persons whom she trusted, persons who could surround her with love and care, persons who would not leave her alone during the final days, persons who would not leave her alone when they had every reason to believe she would give in to her fear and despair. A stronger moral community, stronger and richer moral relationships were needed far earlier in Diane's life than when she was diagnosed with leukemia.

Conclusions

What can we draw from this brief reflection on complex moral decision-making? What are the elements of moral discernment that Scotus would highlight for us today?

The first would be this, **Be expansive and inclusive**! Widen the moral situation, create a larger circle of members, of options, of viewpoints. Moral decision-making is not simply a function of personal autonomy and individual rights. Diane's life and final days might have been more peaceful if others around her had helped her to see beyond the narrow set of options she viewed, because of her despair and fears.

A second moral element might be **Emotions are morally relevant**! Diane, the doctor, her husband and son all seemed to put their emotions away as they attempted to deal with this situation. Diane was content on "maintaining control" right up to the end. Diane's husband and son left her alone when she asked them to leave. What were they feeling? Where was their connection? Dr. Quill refused to listen to his "gut" – he gave her what she wanted. And yet, Diane's negative emotional state was really driving the entire situation.

A third moral element would be **Be Creative**! Don't play things conservatively … take moral risks! Diane's family could have acted more dramatically to build and sustain their relationships with her. They could have stepped forward and attempted to acted on her behalf. Everyone in this situation was passive; Diane was in total control. This was not healthy for her, nor was it a harmonious communal scenario. Who was acting in such a way that beauty was brought to birth in this situation?

A fourth moral element would be **Be faithful**! At a certain point, Diane was abandoned by those around her. Left to herself, she entered into the despair, to the realm of hopelessness. She acted in the best way she could, but where were the others?

A final moral element would be **Know when to act**! Everyone in this situation remained passive, throughout the entire development of the illness. What was her husband thinking? What was he doing? Where were the moral artisans in this situation? The most significant action was taken by Dr. Quill, when he falsified the medical report. Why, if he had acted well, did he need to lie?

For the feminist thinkers whose voices began our reflection and for Scotus, the moral person stands at the center of the moral discussion, both as agent and as object of love and care. But the moral person is not understood as the autonomous agent, but rather as the person in relationship to others and within a community affected deeply by her choices and actions. Scotus offers a vision that is both personalized and creative. It seeks to promote the development of moral persons who are sensitive to beauty around them and alert to the opportunities for creative response in particular situations. His theory calls for the highest level of personal and intellectual training and development, better to hear the Spirit's now. Such moral artisans can be creators of beauty in the world.

In her *Speaking from the Heart* Rita Manning identifies the modern moral goal as the development of the unencumbered self.[28] Diane was certainly an example of this independent, autonomous, objective moral agent. This is the self capable of objective judgment, of standing back and assessing a situation, or so she thought. This notion of the self is found both in Kantian and Utilitarian discussions. Such a self has only one purpose: to become the autonomous moral agent, capable of free decisions and of defending his or her rights in any situation. In the context of libertarian models of freedom, such a self is limited only by the exercise of others in their search for freedom and happiness. Susan Sherman writes, "Within feminist ethics, there is a widespread criticism of the assumption that the role of ethics is to clarify obligations among individuals who are viewed as paradigmatically equal, independent, rational and autonomous."[29]

Scotus, too, sees the moral order as going beyond the individual self to point toward communion and relationship, with others but ultimately with God. In this, his Christian and Franciscan identity plays a key role. Understanding God as

---

[28] A term she borrows from Michael Sandel. See *Speaking from the Heart*, 2-4.

[29] "Feminist and Medical Ethics: Two Different Approaches to Contextual Ethics," 21.

Triune Communion, he sees participation in divinity as the true human goal. This goal is ultimately a deep relationship of love based upon the nature of God as source of reality. Relationship is the moral goal because the divine is essentially relational, because we are created in the image of God, and because we are invited to enter freely into that relationship. This type of Trinitarian foundation has clear implications for an environmental ethic as well.

Scotus frames the moral discussion according to an aesthetic model, both visual and musical in its development. Goodness, like beauty, attracts the natural affection within the will to love generously. In his work, *The Glory of the Lord*, Hans Urs von Balthasar has argued that a culture that loses a sense of what is beautiful is drawn to forget both what is true and what is good.[30] If this is indeed the case, then any attempt to engage in contemporary discussion on moral matters would do well to consider an approach that begins not with moral obligations, with laws or rules, but rather with beauty as foundational to the morally good life. The purpose of moral living might best be understood as the formation of artisans capable of bringing forth beauty in the contingent order, thus expressing their freedom and creativity in imitation of God. This attractive artistic approach could indeed provide the basis for a rich and fruitful reflection on the moral domain, conceived not merely as a dimension of absolute principle, but as the integration of what is best in rational human loving and spiritual aspirations.[31]

---

[30] Hans Urs von Balthasar, *The Glory of the Lord* (San Francisco: Ignatius Press, 1989), 19.

[31] I develop this in much greater detail throughout my work, *The Harmony of Goodness: Mutuality and Moral Living According to John Duns Scotus* (Quincy, IL: Franciscan Press, 1996).

AUTHORS

Brian V. Johnstone, C.Ss.R., is the Warren Blanding Professor of Religion and Culture at The Catholic University of America. He is a moral theologian with interests in fundamental moral theology, bioethics, and peace and war. His research interests include moral theology and philosophy. He is a member of the Redemptorist Congregation.

Thomas A. Shannon is Professor of Religion and Social Ethics in the Department of Humanities and Arts at Worcester Polytechnic Institute, Worcester, MA. He is the author or editor of over twenty books and forty articles in the areas of bioethics and Roman Catholic Social Ethics. His most recent works have been on genetic engineering and include the edited collection *Genetic Engineering: The Documentary History* (Greenwood Press, 1999) and *Made in Whose Image? Genetic Engineering and Christian Ethics* (Humanity Books, 1999).

Kathryn Getek is a doctoral candidate in Theology at Boston College in the area of Theological Ethics. Her current dissertation research is on justice as it relates to the American prison and virtue ethics. She currently holds the Catherine of Siena Teaching Fellowship in Ethics at Villanova University.

Thomas Nairn, O.F.M., is a member of the Sacred Heart Province of the Order of Friars Minor. He currently is the Erica and Harry John Family Professor of Catholic Ethics Director of Health Care Mission Leadership. He received his M.A., and M.Div. at Catholic Theological Union, his Ph.D. from the University of Chicago. He has studied abroad at the University of Cambridge.

Although interested in a wide range of ethical issues, most of Thomas Nairn's research has been in the area of health care ethics. His current work has been in areas such as end of life issues, genetics, the interrelation between religious and cultural values in health care decision making, and organizational ethics. He consults for a variety of Catholic health care systems and helped develop the health care mission leadership certificate program.

Mary Beth Ingham, C.S.J., is Professor of Philosophy and Director of the Honors Program at Loyola Marymount University, Los Angeles. She received her Ph.D. in Philosophy from the University of Fribourg, Switzerland and has taught philosophy at LMU for the past eighteen years. She is the author of seven books and numerous articles on the thought of Franciscan John Duns Scotus (1265-1308). She has been a member of the summer faculty at the Franciscan Institute, St. Bonaventure University and a popular speaker with various Franciscan groups.